19323754

News reporters
and news sources

NEWS REPORTERS AND NEWS SOURCES

Accomplices in shaping and misshaping the news

SECOND EDITION

HERBERT STRENTZ

IOWA STATE UNIVERSITY PRESS / AMES

To my wife, Joan, and our daughters, Tami and Laura,
who may not always be news sources,
but always are sources of encouragement and pride.

Herbert Strentz is Professor of Journalism at Drake University, Des Moines, Iowa.

© 1989 Iowa State University Press, Ames, Iowa 50010
All rights reserved

Manufactured in the United States of America

Second edition, 1989

International Standard Book Number: 0–8138–1886–9 (cloth)
0–8138–1887–7 (paper)

Library of Congress Cataloging-in-Publication Data

Strentz, Herbert.
News reporters and news sources: accomplices in shaping and misshaping the news / Herbert Strentz. — 2nd ed.
p. cm.
Bibliography: p.
Includes index.
ISBN 0–8138–1886–9
ISBN 0–8138–1887–7 (pbk.)
1. Press—United States—Influence. 2. Reporters and reporting—United States—History. 3. Journalism—United States—Objectivity. 4. Journalism—Social aspects—United States. 5. Journalistic ethics—United States. I. Title.
PN4731.S75 1989
070.4′3—dc19
89–1906

Contents

Preface

This book is about what happens *before* news stories are written or broadcast. Such stories do not take form when a reporter sits at a word processor or in front of a microphone. What news will reach the audience has been decided long before the first word is written or spoken — not as a matter of fate or predestination but as a matter of the competence of the reporter and the nature of the reporter's relationship with the news source. The reporter and news source are, as the subtitle of this book suggests, accomplices — often unintentionally — in determining the content of the news.

This second edition is somewhat longer than the first, but not because in the intervening years many answers have been found to the questions confronting the reporter, the source, and the audience. To the contrary, more questions have been asked, more problems discovered. So, more space is devoted to news coverage of terrorism and to ethical issues involved in reporting on the ways that people live and die. The second edition also reflects changes in news-coverage trends. Journalists now cover more aspects of the private lives of public figures, but also appear to provide more protection for the private lives of people who are thrust into the news because of accidents, crime, or other misfortune.

Common to the first and second editions, however, is a measure of confidence and trust that an informed society is healthier than one based on rumors, gossip, and suspicion. That should be true even when the information to be shared by the news reporters and news sources is discomforting or distressing. Also common is the hope that the book can help make the reporter, the news source, and the news audience more sensitive to the nuances of the reporting process, helping us all to better understand and cope with the pressures and joys of a free society — a fitting way to continue into a third century the celebration of the bicentennial of the Bill of Rights and the First Amendment on December 15, 1991.

Thanks are due to the students and colleagues who have contributed to this book in many ways, with particular debt to H. Henry Milam of the Drake University faculty and to graduate assistants Mark Bergsma and John Easley, to the staff of the Iowa State University Press and copy editor Richard Miller, and to Drake University for providing the sabbatical that made the second edition possible. Also, I appreciate the support and interest of those individuals and news organizations who gave permission to use some of their material in this second edition, with special thanks to the editors of the Columbia Journalism Review and the Quill.

Never kill a question

Never kill a question.
It is a fragile thing.
A good question deserves to live.
One doesn't so much answer it as converse with it.
Great questions are permanent and blessed gifts of the mind.
But the greatest questions of all
are those which build bridges to the heart
addressing the whole person.
No answer should be designed to kill the question.
When one is too dogmatic, or too sure,
one shows disrespect for truth
and the question which points toward it.
Beyond my answer there is always more,
more light waiting to break in
and waves of inexhaustible meaning
ready to break against wisdom's widening shore.
Wherever there is a question let it live.

Reprinted by permission from BLESS MY GROWING
by Gerhard Frost
Copyright © 1974 Augsburg Publishing House

1 The influence and power of news

What you see is not necessarily what you get

Introduction

News reporters have much in common with the person in the generic shooting accident who "didn't know the gun was loaded." News and commentary on the printed page, on television, and over radio take unexpected turns that even reporters find surprising, shocking, or distressing. The loaded-gun analogy springs from three key points of this chapter:

1. *News content is not the same as news influence.* The power of the press, popularly translated as the power to shape opinions and to bring about action in a desired direction, should not be understood solely in terms of the content of the news media — news coverage, pronouncements of columnists and commentators, editorial comment, and advertisements. There is more to influence than what meets the eye or is heard by the ear. We experience the subtleties of influence on an interpersonal level when, despite what we say or write, our message is either misunderstood or understood too clearly because of our body language and previous messages or, quite simply, because the other person's mind was made up beforehand.

2. *The way news is collected helps determine what is reported.* The way a reporter gathers information helps determine what insights news sources provide and what information is shared with the audience. The news-gathering process is part of the influence and the power of the press. The distinction between the effects of

the process and the effects of the story is an important one. In sharing information with news sources or as an intermediary between news sources, a reporter may exercise influence without ever writing or producing the news item. The reporter's roles as informant and intermediary are surprisingly common, particularly when so much newsroom emphasis is on the news source as the supposed authority for what is printed or broadcast.

3. *Potential consequences of coverage are weak criteria for news decision making.* One of the most difficult lessons for a reporter to learn is that in deciding whether to cover an event or issue, the possible consequences of such coverage are among the least reliable criteria for decision making. Consequences of the story usually are beyond the control of the reporter. The accuracy and the relative interest and importance of the news item to readers and viewers are more within the bounds of judgments that reporters and editors are qualified to make. Not reporting an event or issue because of imagined harm it might do is likely to lead to little reporting at all. On the other hand, reporting an event or issue because of the *good* it will do is likely to lead to disappointment. That is why the reporter is better advised to think in terms of accuracy and context and in terms of a story's immediacy, prominence, and proximity than in terms of good or bad news. That is a difficult lesson to learn because, for one thing, reporters may want a story to have specific consequences and, for another, much of the pressure that reporters receive from news sources and from the audience is concerned with potential harmful consequences of news stories.

Miss Peach / By Mell Lazarus

Courtesy Mell Lazarus and Field Newspaper Syndica

News content, power, and influence

The phrase "the power of the press" is a bit dated, referring as it does literally to the print medium. It may be a bit misleading, too, because *power* often connotes a degree of formal and organized control to effect change, whereas *influence* may be subtle, indirect, or unintended.

The connotation of "power" is evident in the reference and reverence to the press as the "Fourth Branch of Government,"[1] according it a place in the separation of powers doctrine in the U.S. Constitution, along with the executive, legislative, and judicial branches. The "influence" approach, for purposes of this discussion, places upon the sovereign public—the ultimate seat of power—the responsibility to act on information provided by the news media and other social institutions, such as home, church, and school. The difference in these two connotations, while neither neat nor easily separable, is reflected in the ways that different reporters work with news sources and in the differing approaches they take to their news stories.

For example, Clark Mollenhoff, who won a Pulitzer Prize for his reporting on corruption in the Teamsters Union, is an unabashed advocate of the power of the press. He would likely consider a story that he wrote about corruption in government to be a failure unless someone was fired, went to jail, or paid other penalties for violations of the law. Mollenhoff would work with prosecuting attorneys, sharing information and coordinating efforts, all in the interest of getting the "bad guys." (Asked once how he kept his spirits up, even though despite his reporting and the efforts of others corruption still flourished in government, he replied in effect: "Oh, I think about that once in a while, and then when I start shaving in the morning I think about all the money being spent in government and all the records to check and all the things going on and I start shaving faster and faster and can't wait until I get to work".)

In similar fashion a governmental agency might accord a television station the "opportunity" to work with the government in getting a bad guy. A TV news crew might work with the police by surreptitiously filming an insurance scam. Undercover agents are wired for sound and filmed as they buy a fraudulent insurance policy from a suspect who hopes to pocket a premium payment before the customers realize that the policy does not offer the promised coverage. The payoffs: the police get filmed evidence, and the station gets a great item for the evening newscast – police and criminals in action.

Many journalists would balk at working hand in glove with news sources, arguing that reporters are not private investigators and that it is the responsibility of the news media to report the news and the responsibility of the police and prosecuting attorneys to catch the bad guys. For these journalists the reporter's duties end with the publication of the story; in fact, they argue that working closely with government officials might jeopardize relationships with other news sources. In the insurance scam example, they would be fearful that cooperation with the police would raise questions about subsequent coverage of the suspect's trial and about who would have ownership of the videotape should the operation not go as planned and the undercover agents misbehave or the suspect become violent. Therefore, not only would such journalists not work with government news sources at the onset of an investigation, but they would keep their distance afterward, fighting in court to keep reporters from testifying at a trial or from providing unpublished or unbroadcast material to either side in a legal case. In this approach journalistic cooperation would be limited to providing a deposition stating that what was printed or broadcast was accurate, to the best of the reporter's knowledge.[2]

It is not always easy to distinguish between *working with* and *reporting on* news sources. Respect for a news reporter rests more on the accuracy and completeness of the news story than on the reporter's style of gathering information. The reporter must be sensitive, however, to any relationship with news sources that lessens the journalist's control of news content or threatens credibility with the audience and other news sources. The arms-length approach poses fewer problems.

MIXED AND UNCERTAIN RESULTS

Newspapers and television stations cover a governor's seemingly endless mistakes, and an effort to recall him through a new election helps drive him from office; a series of television programs on child abuse is followed by state legislation requiring physicians and school teachers to report any suspicious case; the city planning commission denies a request to rezone land after a news story raises questions about the land developer's contributions to a city councilman's campaign; in reviewing receipts picked up in a vice squad raid on a local massage parlor, a reporter notes the name of a respected public official as one of the customers, and the news story is followed by the official's resignation.

All these are examples of the impact of the press, right? Now consider a few other examples.

When news stories correctly report that a police chief interfered with a burglary investigation in which his son was a suspect, the chief is mildly reprimanded, but policemen who talked to the reporter are suspended from duty; a newspaper's editorial campaign about problems with the county jail is followed by the resounding defeat of a bond issue for a new facility; less than 25 percent of the registered voters go to the polls in an election that the news media report is critical to the future of the city's schools; blood donations decline despite a public relations campaign to assure prospective donors that they will not risk infection with AIDS (acquired immune deficiency syndrome). The surprise to editors and reporters in this second group of cases may be that the "loaded gun" did *not* go off, that well-documented news coverage of social problems and political issues did not generate concern to work for solutions, to respond in informed fashion. Such developments leave reporters talking to themselves and provide editors a sardonic chuckle when they hear themselves referred to as being among the most powerful people in the community. Why doesn't the gun go off?

A simplistic view. One reason for confusion regarding the power and influence of the press is a too simplistic view of the reporting process. Something happens after a news item is written or broadcast; therefore, it is argued, it happened because of the news item. The problem is compounded because it is not widely appreciated that the news media serve as societal mirrors far more often than they serve as visionaries or prophets. If the news media appear to have power or influence, it may be because they are faithfully reporting the directions in which society itself is moving.

The relatively simplistic view of the effects of the media springs, in part, from early communication theory, which was influenced by the apparent direct effects of British and German propaganda machines in the two world wars. The so-called hypodermic theory depicted a process in which a passive public was "injected" with information. Later a two-step flow communication theory developed, which recognized that people generally turned to others for insight and leadership; in the first step, information in the media might reach opinion leaders on various subjects who, in the second step, would influence others who might turn to them for advice. An agenda-setting approach to media influence suggests that although the media may not directly influence what people think, the news media do set an agenda for what people talk about and discuss. None of the theories, of course, is universally applicable, but preference here is given to the interpretations that look for subtler media effects.

Still, the content-equals-influence argument is a popular one, reinforced by people who keep scrapbooks to show how much attention their cause, candidate, or corporation received in the news media. Such practices persist even though people may hold opinions despite—not because of—the content of news stories.

Don't confuse me, my mind's made up. Much of what we do—what we read, where we go to church, whom we talk with, study with, and socialize with—reinforces beliefs. Since we seldom go out of our way to find someone disagreeable, anyone seeking to get us to do something different or to change our minds is confronting not just a particular issue but our lifestyles.

In some cases, the more evidence that is accumulated against our point of view, the more we cling tenaciously to it. Disconfirming evidence may only strengthen an opinion. Consider the saga of television evangelists Jim and Tammy Bakker. With all the critical stories and hard evidence about their misbehavior, one would think their flock would scatter. But a 67-year-old believer told the *Orlando Sentinel*, " 'It's nothing new. That old Satan, he knows where to go. Satan, he's after all the preachers that are winning — Oral Roberts, Rex Humbard.' "[3] And another news source declared, " 'There is no way Jim Bakker has been in any old motel with a woman in Florida. His heart is pure. But if it's true, we'll just pray him back straight.' "[4] The more evidence accumulated against the Bakkers, the more it became clear that they were successful preachers whom Satan was trying to destroy. Similarly, other beliefs and behavior might be reinforced — even if apparently wrong — because a person is persuaded that an outcome would have been markedly worse had not he or she persevered. Journalists who advocate openness in government, for example, counter arguments about the problems of openness by contending that any outcome produced in secrecy would only be worse.

Nothing is as popular as an easy answer.   The notion that news coverage influences the outcome of an issue or event has merit. Few deny that the news media sometimes can shape events through what is reported in the news or advocated in an editorial. But the news media more often have the effect of setting an agenda for discussion and contributing to the general outcome. That is a far cry from giving the news media credit for ousting a president or getting a bond issue passed. Still, the tangible nature of news coverage, the linking of news coverage of an event with the outcome of the event, and the search for someone to blame or someone to credit make the news media a convenient scapegoat or hero. Besides, the press is not unwilling to wear the mantle of hero or to bear the blame for misfortune that is considered part of the price for protecting First Amendment freedoms. For better or worse, however, much of the impact of the press on society is far more subtle and indirect.

The reporter as informant and as intermediary

To fully appreciate the role of the news media in our society, one should recognize that the journalist often has an effect even when editorials, columns, or news stories are neither written nor read, neither broadcast nor heard. Simply by talking with news sources, by gathering information, a reporter may shape the outcome of a newsworthy event or issue.

INFORMING NEWS SOURCES

Sometimes a reporter is shocked when it is necessary to tell a news source something the source was presumed to have known. In a boating accident off the California coast a man drowns and several others are injured. Hours later a reporter for an inland newspaper phones the home of the drowning victim, expecting the person who answers the phone to be upset. If the victim's family is too distraught, maybe a neighbor or a cousin will be at home and will be able to provide the information, the reporter thinks. The reporter's phone call, however, is greeted with a cheery hello. Instead of getting information for an obituary about the victim, it is the reporter who breaks the news of the accident to the family and who provides them with a sheriff's office phone number to call for further information. A private plane crash in a distant state kills a local woman. The local reporter reads the Associated Press story about the crash and then phones the victim's home for additional information. He does not get the information, however, because no one at home knew about the accident. Understandably, the reporter is asked to phone back later.

These instances dramatically illustrate the role of the reporter in providing information to people presumed to be news sources. Roles and rules are changed. Instead of being the fact-gathering reporter, the newsperson provides information in a way and at a moment that the news source will remember forever. How does one do this? Coroners and medical examiners who have shared news of grief thousands of times say there is no formula to make such news less traumatic. The reporter plainly must be sympathetic and compassionate, providing information and expressing regrets. It may be advisable to determine whether the news source is alone or perhaps even to contact a neighbor, relative, or clergyman to assist the bereaved. It does no good to hang up the phone or to cut the conversation short and not share at least some information with the news source. A reporter might ask some questions, depending upon the circumstances, or make arrangements to visit or call back later or to phone someone else.

Such an exchange of roles is uncomfortable for the reporter.[5] Accustomed to gathering information and transmitting it to an impersonal news audience, the reporter suddenly becomes the news source, providing information to the very people who are supposed to tell what has happened. Isn't that what reporting is all about?

No, not really. Reporters often disclose their opinions, views, and expectations inadvertently, as will be discussed in upcoming chapters, and sometimes reporters share information not so inadvertently. With the emphasis on specialized reporting that developed in the 1970s, reporters have become valued sources of information for public officials who seek solutions to difficult problems.

Donald Bolles, an investigative reporter for the *Arizona Republic* of Phoenix was killed in 1976 by a bomb rigged to his car. Presumably Bolles knew too much about land fraud schemes in Arizona, about which he had testified before the Select Committee on Crime of the U.S. House of Representatives. His reporting had made him an expert on ties between organized crime and dog racing in Arizona. Bolles's death gave impetus to the growth of Investigative Reporters and Editors, Inc. (IRE), which he had helped found the year before. A volunteer task force of journalists went to Arizona to complete a series of articles on Bolles's work and to demonstrate that reporters would not be intimidated.

James Risser, a reporter for the *Des Moines Register,* did not testify before a Congressional committee, although he had won a Pulitzer Prize for reporting about corruption in grain exporting. He acknowledged that he felt uneasy when congressmen asked his opinion on pending legislation and other proposals to combat corruption. He was uneasy because of what he saw as the danger of his becoming a participant in a news story he was covering. His solution was to discuss alternatives open to Congress and to share insights with public officials, but he stopped well short of advocating public policy to those who were his news sources.

Bolles and Risser had at least two advantages not always available to reporters working with news sources: they knew that the people they were talking with were seeking information that might be used at a later time, and they had options as to whether they would answer questions and, if they did answer, to what extent they would provide the information and opinions desired.

As court records of recent years demonstrate, however, reporters sometimes are asked for information under threat of being jailed if they do not comply with court orders. The specialization of reporters and the access of many of them to dissident groups in society have tempted grand juries, attorneys general, police, and other public officials to seek information from reporters through subpoena, contempt proceedings, or other legal avenues. Such new definitions of the newsreporter–news source relationship are both symbol and sign of the changing roles of reporters in our society.

A far less dramatic but more pervasive role of the reporter as informant occurs as the reporter constructs a dialogue between news sources. Indeed, this role is so common that reporters and news sources accept it often with only a passing thought about the risks and trust that it entails. In this relationship the reporter gets information from one news source and later asks another news source to respond to the first source's comments. Typically such dialogues are constructed by the reporter on controversial and relatively fast-breaking news stories. The reporter may work back and forth between news sources or involve third and fourth sources in the discussion, again with none of the sources talking directly with one another.

The assumptions involved in such transactions reflect either the trust that a news source may have in a reporter's competence or a news source's desire to get a point of view across, or a little of both. The second and third news sources, if they respond to the reporter's request for comment, assume that the reporter is quoting or paraphrasing the original news source correctly and in context. They assume, too, that the reporter is not misleading them, intentionally or unintentionally, simply to develop a better story, and that their comments, based on the reporter's question, speak to the heart of an issue and not to some easily rebuttable, tangential issue. It is a fascinating process, partly because it is taken for granted. The process may strengthen reporter–news source ties, because many news sources welcome the opportunity to offer timely comment. But the process can also damage those ties if subsequent sources feel they have been misled by the reporter and if their comments, offered in good faith, are wide of the mark hit by the first source.

The reporter is vulnerable in the process, too, because even if his or her work is accurate and complete, news sources may patch over differences by saying that the supposed misunderstanding was fabricated by the press. That is part of the risk the news reporter takes in playing the role of informant.

THE REPORTER AS INTERMEDIARY

The reporter may serve as an intermediary between different news sources, just as the reporter in the more familiar role is an intermediary between news sources and the news audience.

The role of intermediary may be most visible in smaller communities where the reporter or editor daily meets with news sources on social, religious, and professional bases. The small-town editor may have influence in his community because he regularly talks with all the community leaders, even if the substance of their conversations is never published. A longtime North Dakota journalist, Paul Schmidt, said that when he was an editor in Enderlin, he knew that one councilman would get a good idea from him, have the city council act on it, and then take the credit when the item was reported and supported in the newspaper.

The same thing happens in larger cities, where reporters may talk with several decision makers within a week, pollinating one with ideas from another. Indeed, a reporter may talk more with government agencies than the agencies talk with each other.

Government agencies at the city, county, state, and federal levels at times almost make it a point to act independently, even though they all are doing so supposedly in the interest of the same person—the taxpayer. Grand schemes might be drawn up for industrial development or for state recreation areas in Kentucky with little concern for similar programs in the contiguous states of Illinois, Indiana, Ohio, West Virginia, Tennessee, and Missouri. Or, on a smaller scale, city planners in Bakersfield, California, might think of city development without considering what Kern County planners have in mind for zoning just outside the Bakersfield city limits.

The way news coverage is assigned is sometimes more logical than the way government agencies operate. In Bakersfield whoever covers the city planning agency for *The Californian*, the local newspaper, may also cover county planning. If so, the county and city planners will talk to each other at least through the reporter. Contradictions in city and county plans may be discovered, discussed, and remedied without a story's ever being written. The reporter may not even know contradictions exist, but may—by simply stopping by the courthouse and talking for a while with the county planner—share information necessary for the county to have if there is to be intelligent land development where city and county lines meet.

The reporter may also be used by news sources to serve as a knowing or unknowing intermediary. Hodding Carter, whose credentials include work as a newspaper editor, a U.S. State Department spokesman, and a press critic, has observed:

> The reporter is in a position of supplicant. You—the source—have something he wants: information. But if you, as an official, look at it only in that way, then you're in trouble because he also has something you want: access to the public. And it's important to remember that reporters also provide sources with a conduit enabling them to get their messages across to their adversaries and their allies.[6]

The reporter's role as an intermediary seldom has been etched as starkly as it was when Tom Wicker of the *New York Times* went to Attica Prison in upstate New York in 1971. Wicker was one of several persons whom rebelling prisoners had invited to Attica to negotiate between them and prison authorities. Wicker tells of that painful episode in his reporting career in his book *A Time to Die* (Quadrangle/New York Times). Forty-three persons, including hostages, were killed — all but one by police gunfire — when the negotiations failed and the prison yard was recaptured by force.

Wicker's visibility as an intermediary at Attica helped preclude any misuse or abuse of his role as a reporter. Readers were plainly forewarned of his involvement. More often, however, the reporter's role as intermediary or informant is involuntary, subtle, or inadvertent.

Reporters must at times share information with news sources — educate them, if you will — to get a more informed response to questions that should be answered for the news audience. The reporter is not a mere transmission belt, taking information from one source and passing it along to another, but a participant in an important and complex communication process. To the extent the reporter is sensitive to how he or she influences what happens in that process, the news audience will be better served.

The intermediary as surrogate decision maker or social worker. How does one distinguish between the role of the reporter as intermediary and the role of the reporter as do-gooder? When anyone talks about a reporter exercising influence without ever writing a news story, the next step is a predictable one: the primary role of the reporter might in that case be interpreted as the solving of social problems and the resolution of political conflicts. If a reporter can remedy difficult situations without writing a story, why not do so? The role is a tempting one for three reasons:

1. The reporter may decide that the ultimate goal of journalism is to improve society and make the world a more manageable, caring place — even by as simple a move as increasing a state or city budget to subsidize day-care facilities for the children of working

parents. If solely the response of an informed public is to be relied on, such improvements will take a lot longer to implement than if the reporter can be a "surrogate public" and lobby for change without necessarily writing news stories day in and day out.

2. For the reporter there is a heady feeling that comes from being near the center of power — whether that center is something as modest as a small-town zoning commission or as awesome as the U.S. President's National Security Council. When one becomes a confidant or even just an acquaintance of people wielding power, it is easy to understand the troubles they face and to cooperate with them. One joins the team and relishes the role of being an intermediary between contending centers of power.

3. Most news sources believe, rightly or wrongly, that they understand the "big picture" better than others, and they may fear that the "power of the press" could botch up grand programs. A wrong story here, a misplaced quote there, and *voila* — the reporter has killed a program that offered great potential for the betterment of society. A reporter who has been cautioned by a news source as to the great harm that could result from an incomplete or ill-informed news story may well decide that it is in everyone's best interest to leave the story unwritten. Even more tempting is a compromise to delay a news report until the risk of any potential damage has passed.

Consequences of news stories

The gap between reporters and the news audience and news sources is widest when discussions turn to the harmful consequences of news stories. Printed and broadcast news accounts are blamed for damaging reputations, ruining or even costing lives, tarnishing the image of the local high school, hurting the chances of the community to attract new industry, encouraging criminal activity, invading privacy, being insensitive to the concerns of minority groups or persons with physical disabilities, and creating an assortment of other problems. Often these collective evils are summarized under the charge that the news media report too much "bad news."

Journalists respond, in part, that they only report what is news, that people want to kill the messenger because the news is bad, and that the First Amendment gives them the right to tell what is happening in society.[7] Reasons for such differences of opinion include the following:

1. To the news reporter, controversy often constitutes news and is not necessarily good or bad. Controversy may be viewed as an index of a healthy society that recognizes and addresses its problems. To news sources and others, including public officials and educators, controversy is bad; it is taken as evidence that the system is not working or is viewed as something contrived by the news media. As one observer noted, "I fear a significant factor in the tattered image of the press is caused by the public's perception that nothing is too trivial for us to blow up."[8]

2. To buttress entries in journalism contests, editors and news directors will point to legislation or other reforms that followed news accounts of corruption or social problems. If the news media take the credit for such direct consequences, critics contend, shouldn't they also take the blame when things go wrong?

3. The news media are an available target both for those seeking to understand complex social issues and for those trying to avoid responsibility for problems they have created or sustained. Routinely blame is placed on the press and "outside agitators" for controversy resulting from such episodes as civil rights violations, objections to prayers at public-school graduation ceremonies, and discussion of the private lives of public officials.

4. People may endure problems or unfortunate events but object when those problems or events are validated through news coverage that shares information with a broader community. For example, the consequences of a drunk-driving arrest are blamed on a news report of the arrest and not on the driver. Or the impact of a divorce is believed to be made worse because of a news account based on court records. The routine news process in which matters of public record are reported seems to legitimize and expand problems that those involved would just as soon forget and put behind them.

5. The impact of the news media often is overstated, and the news audience is too readily defined as powerless. Citizens do not have to vote the way a newspaper editorial suggests; they can still support a candidate even though a news story implies the person is untrustworthy because of pending criminal indictments. It is easier to focus, however, on potential dire consequences of a news report than to gauge the responses of a disparate news audience.

6. The news media themselves believe that some news coverage may have harmful consequences. For example, when the U.S. stock market plunged an incredible five hundred points on October 19, 1987, "many editors banished [the term] The Crash from headlines and body copy because they feared the term might increase market panic"[9] by linking this crash to the one that introduced the Great Depression in 1929. Similar concerns are routinely discussed in newsrooms—if not to avoid harmful consequences then to consider the likelihood that the nature of the news coverage may affect the outcome of an event.

7. Finally, the impact of mass media coverage of issues is at best incompletely understood. A 1986 article in the *New England Journal of Medicine* reported that there appeared to be an increase in suicide attempts among teenagers in the wake of four television programs dealing with teenage suicide, although it was not determined whether the teenagers involved had actually viewed any of the programs.[10] The coverage of teen suicides had been conscientious, perhaps even laudable, and in some cases resembled a classroom discussion. The dilemma is clear: to ignore concerns about teenage suicide would be irresponsible, but to report on it might encourage imitative behavior, if the researchers are right. In this case, however, there was clear-cut evidence of concern about the issue, and those concerns simply could not be swept under the rug. We should not be fearful of telling one another what is happening in our society.

Even with the understandable reasons for focusing on the potential consequences of news stories, the point of this chapter remains that such consequences are not good criteria for deciding whether to report about some issue, event, or individual. That is because news reporters are more competent to determine the accuracy, context, and credibility of a news story or news source than they are to predict the future. Generally the reporter, news sources, and news audience are better served if news coverage decisions are based on questions of accuracy and context rather than on imagined consequences.

Trying to be Mr. or Ms. Fix-It. In simple classroom exercises or discussions it is easy to see how willing students are to adopt the role of Mr. or Ms. Fix-It. Pose a problem in which a reporter is asked to not report a story because (1) someone may be harmed or (2) the problem can be solved just as readily without the notoriety a story might bring. More often than not, the student agrees to not write the story.

A problem: James Hennings, a 32-year-old furniture salesman, was arrested ten days ago on a burglary charge. The paper carried a story about his arrest. Now the charges have been dropped, and a follow-up story seems warranted. But his wife phones an assistant editor and argues: "Do you have to print another story? Jim's boss at work really was upset about the story on the burglary arrest, but he's calmed down now. He's willing to keep Jim on the job if there is no more publicity about the whole thing. It was a mistake anyway—Jim was just getting back some furniture we had stored with people. If you print the story about the charges having been dropped, the whole thing will blow up again and Jim will be fired. We just can't afford to lose this job. Jim's worked so hard. Please don't print the story." What do you tell Mrs. Hennings?

A common classroom answer is to ask for the boss's phone number so the reporter can take Jim off the hook and make things easier for him at work. Another answer is to check out the case and do an investigative job on what led to the dismissal of charges. Then if it appears that Jim is indeed innocent, don't write the story, but if something is fishy, go ahead and write it.

It occurs to almost no students that Mrs. Hennings may be

lying, or that whether she is lying or whether Jim is "really" guilty is irrelevant to the decision about running the story. Nor does it occur to many that a phone call may be just the thing to convince the publicity-shy boss that Hennings should have been fired right after the arrest.

If the paper has run a story about the arrest, it must run the story about charges being dropped. There is a responsibility to the readers and to the record and even to the Hennings family. The possible consequences of not printing the second story include lingering questions in readers' minds about when Hennings will go to trial and possible errors two or three years later when a different reporter, working on another story about Hennings, finds only the clipping about his arrest. Such possibilities are at least as injurious as any imagined consequences from the boss's seeing the story that charges against his employee have been dropped.

The harmful consequences of nonpublication are not limited to routine matters like police reports. For example, President John F. Kennedy pleaded concern for national security to dissuade the *New York Times* from reporting all it knew about plans for the 1961 Bay of Pigs assault against Fidel Castro's Cuba. After the invasion became a military fiasco, Kennedy told the newspaper's editors, "Maybe if you had printed more about the operation you would have saved us from a colossal mistake."[11]

Hindsight is twenty-twenty. But in making news judgments, reporters, editors, and news directors may find themselves tied in knots if they consider all the possible consequences of the stories they plan to publish or broadcast.

The problem is that there is no news story that cannot possibly harm or upset someone. To take from a newspaper, a broadcast, or even our day-to-day conversations any information that might have adverse or unintended consequences would leave the newspaper blank, the airwaves silent, and our conversations in limbo.

Glance through a newspaper, a company newsletter, a church bulletin, or a television broadcast for "harmless" information. Many items will appear harmless: a short obituary about a 75-year-old man who led a full life; an engagement announcement; an item about finalists for homecoming king and queen. The obituary might spark a family feud about the order in which the surviving children are listed and whether Roy should have been listed at all, since "we all know how Dad felt about him"; the engagement item might surprise some parents with wedding details that they had not heard about; the homecoming story may hurt the egos of some candidates upset by losing to a "nerd."

Exaggerated? Perhaps. But consider the case of a woman who phoned to complain about front-page news coverage of a man who fatally stabbed his brother. The killer also cut his mother when she tried to stop the assault in her kitchen. The woman on the phone was the mother, who had sufficiently recovered from her wound to voice her complaint: the story said she and her mortally wounded son had been taken to the county hospital, whereas in fact they were taken to a private hospital. She did not want readers to think the family was so poor they had to go to the county hospital. At least this unexpected complaint can be explained in part by its source, a grief-stricken mother whose world had been shattered within a few violent minutes in the family kitchen. And, after all, the hospital named in the story was the wrong one.

It is not only the stories of high drama and violence that may have unintended consequences. The *Lexington* (Ky.) *Herald-Leader* ran a feature photo, sort of a filler, on two Detroit twins whose aunt had made them a huge birthday cake. What resulted was a run on baking goods at Lexington supermarkets. Aunts and mothers became upset because the paper, having run the Detroit photo, would not now print photos of gigantic birthday cakes made right in Lexington.

That a reporter cannot anticipate all the consequences of a story does not mean there is a standing invitation or excuse for irresponsible and incomplete news coverage. (Indeed, as noted in chapters 4 and 6, the evidence is to the contrary: the generally thin-skinned news media are becoming more responsive to concerns voiced by news sources and subjects.) The point here is that the news audience is better served if the decision to report on an issue or event is made in terms of the story's interest, importance, and accuracy than in terms of the good or ill that might result.

Summary

Concern with the power and influence of the news media, the role of the reporter as intermediary, and the consequences of news stories should suggest at least that it is useful and probably necessary for reporters, students of reporting, and the news audience to recognize the subtleties and dynamics of the news-gathering process.

Reporters would be more competent and the news audience better informed if they recognized how a reporter gathering information determines what news ultimately reaches the audience, and that even if some information never reaches the audience, the reporter may have influenced the direction of public policy simply by asking questions of people in positions of power and by serving as an intermediary between news sources.

The challenge to the reporter as informant and intermediary is at least twofold. First, the reporter must resist the temptation to become part of the news event at the expense of responsibility to the news audience. Second, the reporter must recognize that the selection of news sources and the questions he or she asks not only will affect the story itself but also may shape the outcome of whatever issue is reported on. Central to both these points is the understanding that the reporter's responsibility is primarily to the news audience, not to the news source. It is small satisfaction if a news source is delighted with coverage that misleads the audience or is pleased because there was no news coverage at all of an event that the audience should have been informed about.

The effects of the way the reporter gathers information and the dynamics of the reporter-source relationship may be unintended, often unperceived, and sometimes unpredictable. Nevertheless, they are real and a part of the power and influence of the press.

2 Pitfalls and pratfalls

Reporters and news sources as accomplices in shaping and misshaping the news

Introduction

In *Dragnet,* a television detective series of a generation ago that has since been recycled on cable television, Jack Webb as Sergeant Joe Friday sought "just the facts." Criminals were caught and crimes solved because of Sgt. Friday's insistence on "just the facts, ma'am," a line that popped up in enough *Dragnet* episodes to be parodied nationwide. Although that method worked well for Sgt. Friday and TV justice, a news reporter suffers delusions and misleads the audience if the reporter thinks there is a collection of information that consists of "just the facts," unaffected by the perceptions of the news source or the way the reporter gathers information.

The reporter, the news source, and the audience will be better served by remembering a few points:

1. Different persons see the same event or issue in different ways.
2. The same source will report the same event selectively and differently depending upon the audience.
3. How "the facts" are reported and the news is shaped depends upon (a) the nature of the news-gathering process, (b) how news is defined, (c) how news is made rational, (d) how news is prejudged, and (e) how the reporter copes with the pressure to produce good stories.

Different views of the same event

Because it is easily understood, the fable about the blind men and the elephant is often used to illustrate how people see things differently. One blind man felt the elephant's legs and likened the beast to a tree; another felt its tail and called it a rope; a third felt its side and recognized that the pachyderm was quite like a wall; the one who felt an ear declared the animal to be a fan; it is more like a spear, said the one who felt a tusk; and the one who felt its trunk knew that if anything the elephant was most like a snake. Each had a version of the truth and, unfortunately, even taken collectively, the versions did not add up to "one elephant."

That fable is both useful and harmless — useful because it makes the point, harmless because it does not arouse the emotional response provoked by a suggestion that people have differing perceptions and interpretations of God, the family, the flag, Mom, and apple pie. What makes much of reporting difficult is that news sources generally do not intend to deceive or mislead the reporter, and the reporter does not intend to mislead the news audience. Like the men in the fable, they give their honest and — to them — accurate perceptions. That those perceptions may change from morning to afternoon or may differ from reporter to reporter usually is not the result of any conspiracy to distort or mislead the reporter and the audience.

People have vested interests, and those interests affect how they see the world. A person does not have to be the incarnation of evil to oppose having women serve in the armed forces; nor does someone have to be a simpleton or a libertine to oppose mandated testing for AIDS. A politician does not have to be a Communist dupe to believe in arms control or detente. A parent does not have to be ignorant to want to ban a school textbook. (Many readers, like the author, might be tempted to add "but it helps" after one or another of these statements — just further evidence of the point we are trying to make.)

Consider, for example, American news coverage of the nuclear-reactor accident at Chernobyl in the Soviet Union in the spring of 1986. One apt assessment of that coverage found it to be exaggerated, sloppy, and nationalistic. American news coverage was shaped by at least three damaging influences: (1) Russian reluctance to disclose unfavorable information, (2) the eagerness of U.S. officials to turn Chernobyl into a propaganda victory, and (3) the willingness of U.S. reporters to use anonymous sources, who often turned out to be wrong.

> The degree to which America's media had been co-opted by officialdom was probably nowhere more apparent than in the NBC reaction to [Soviet leader Mikhail] Gorbachev's . . . speech in which he criticized the media.
> The network didn't rely on anyone from the media for a defense. Instead, NBC reported a statement from the White House, which said any media missteps that might have occurred "were the result of the extreme secrecy by the Kremlin." . . . The White House had become the spokesman for NBC. . . .
> It was almost as if the American media were telling the public that, in situations like this, "you can't necessarily count on us for accuracy." [NBC's Tom] Brokaw made almost the same point . . . when he said, "You ought to [listen to us] with a healthy dose of skepticism."[1]

Skepticism is indeed good advice.

Sometimes it is useful to think of news sources or interest groups as having flags that they wave. The inscriptions on these banners suggest how the news sources view the world. Members of school boards, for example, have a banner that reads "For the Children." When a reporter asks why the school board took a certain action, the members unfurl the flag and announce, "We did it for the children." Labor unions have a flag that reads "For the Workers." From one presidential administration to the next the president and his staff pass along flags that read "For National Security." The flags of many city councils read "For the Community." Boy Scouts do things "For God and Country." Academic deans and provosts do things "For the University." Journalists, of course, do things "For the Public's Right to Know" or, more important, "For the First Amendment," but that's another story. In reporting on school boards, labor unions, and city councils, among others, a reporter who does not take into account the orientation and interests of the news source is likely to feel misled or lied to when encountering other news sources who have credible, opposing — even contradictory — points of view.

Occasionally, one might meet a person of high principle who says, "If you lie to me just once, I'll never trust you again." Few reporters can afford such high principles; in a month's time they would not have anyone to talk with and would be useless to their employers and their audience. Hodding Carter, a former newspaper editor and a spokesman for the administration of President Jimmy Carter, noted that reporters may not have any choice but to deal with occasionally misleading sources: "Reporters will go back to those who have conned them because the ones who count are often the biggest con artists, and you can never be sure that the next time they won't be giving you something that's really important."[2]

Outright lies or biased perceptions may be misleading, and it is not always too easy for the reporter or the news audience to distinguish between them. News sources who mislead a reporter do not always do so deliberately or maliciously.[3]

The point is driven home hundreds of times a day: by copy editors who insist that an address given by the police be checked against the telephone book, city directory, or other sources; by a reporter who still looks in the dictionary for the spelling of a word, even though a newsroom colleague has offered the correct spelling; by reporters who recognize that a plaintiff's interpretation of a court order will differ from the defendant's. As Walter Lippmann noted in his classic essay on stereotypes, "For the most part we do not see and then define, we define and then we see."[4] Or, to paraphrase him, we often see what we want to see and hear what we want to hear.

Different views from the same source

While it is easy to recognize stereotyping behavior at least in others, we may be less sensitive to the notion that the same person may report the same event selectively and differently, depending upon the audience. This further complicates the work of the information gatherer, who now must contend not only with differing reports from different sources, but with differing reports from the same person.

Consider two examples. A school board member might explain a decision to support a $10 million bond issue in different ways to different audiences. To voters it might be presented as a difficult decision calling for sacrifice—unfurl that flag—for the sake of the children. To teachers the bond issue might be presented as a move toward improved teaching facilities and better salaries. To other board members it might be interpreted as opportune because chances for passage of the bond issue appear to be better now than they will be in a few years when the facilities will be most needed. To a spouse the bond issue might be presented as a chance to accomplish something worthwhile, to have something to show after all those years of school board meetings.

A high school student going to the senior prom or homecoming dance might report plans for the event selectively to different persons. With schoolmates the discussion of the prospective date will depend on the date's relative popularity, whether the person being talked with also will be going to the dance, whether the speaker would have preferred to be going with someone else, and whether that is known. With parents different values might be stressed: perhaps the date's thoughtfulness and upbringing and the other couples who will go along with them. Combining these different descriptions of the date might give us a mix of Tom Cruise, Tina Turner, Madonna, Pee Wee Herman, Ann Landers and Jason from the Friday the 13th horror films, and the resultant view of the date may be as accurate as the fable's composite elephant.

In both illustrations the different accounts to different audiences are not necessarily contradictory. But the pictures that different listeners receive are indeed varied, and the sum of all the pictures still may not equal the whole. If accounts of high school dates and bond issues can vary so easily, why should we be surprised when political candidates are reported as saying different things to different audiences or when there are apparently contradictory accounts of other news events?

Such supposed double-talk occurs and disconcerts us for at least two reasons: (1) since we focus so much on what is said we do not adequately take into account the audience and its effect upon the speaker; (2) having already acquainted ourselves with one version of an issue, we now must modify our understanding to accommodate the latest comments. The world becomes a more complex place, and that is unsettling.

Logically, if the audience influences what the speaker says, then the reporter may influence what the news source says in much the same fashion. The news source may respond to a reporter's questions not only in terms of the source's self-interest but also in terms of how the reporter is perceived. Consider three rather obvious cases. If a female reporter is asking citizens for quick comments on federal funds for medical services, including abortions, she is likely to get responses different from those given to a male reporter. If a black or Hispanic reporter is interviewing a city council member about a program to assure that a certain percentage of minority group members is hired by the fire department, that reporter is likely to receive information different from what a white reporter would be told. A reporter who appears sympathetic to a news source's predicament is likely to elicit responses different from those given a reporter who is perceived as neutral or hostile.

It is easy to add to this list. The point is that who the reporter is and how the reporter is perceived by the news source may determine what information reaches the news audience — especially if the reporter is unaware of influences upon the news source and does not take steps to lessen the chances of being misled. These steps include asking follow-up questions, doing homework before an interview, gaining the confidence of the news source, reviewing public records on an issue, and making the news source's perceptions work to the reporter's and the news audience's advantage.

The nature of the news-gathering process

Distortion is inherent in news gathering simply because of condensation of information if not because of problems introduced by news reporters and sources. A five-paragraph obituary covers seventy-five years of a person's life. A four-paragraph story summarizes a three-hour city council meeting. Just as the word "table" is a symbol of the real thing, so a news story is not the real event or issue but a representation of it. The limits of time are constraints to which both the news audience and news reporters need to be sensitive.

A reporter's news-gathering style may change not only from day to day but within a single interview or news-gathering situation. If what a news source tells a reporter depends upon how the reporter is perceived and how the reporter behaves, then a hardworking reporter can use that behavior and those perceptions to reduce the chances of being misled and to limit distortion.

Two good examples of such skillful reporting are found in two television documentaries broadcast almost twenty years apart. In one, Bill Moyers reports on the role of missionaries in the midst of political upheaval and war in Central America.[5] In the other, Jack Perkins provides some insights into the man convicted of killing U.S. Senator Robert F. Kennedy.[6]

In a public television program first broadcast December 9, 1987, Moyers set out to examine conflicts arising because "two visions of Christianity, two views of salvation have come face to face. One encouraged by the United States government, the other vigorously opposed. Christians are choosing sides."

Moyers first interviewed Philip Derstine of Gospel Crusade about support for the Nicaraguan Contra rebels and about the involvement of Lt. Col. Oliver North, an aide to the National Security Council, in helping Gospel Crusade make contact with the Contras. He asked probing questions in a succinct, nonthreatening fashion, providing the viewer with insight into the philosophy of Gospel Crusade:

DERSTINE: You have to realize that the communist mentality is one that says that the end justifies the means, that if I can get away with it, it's okay; as long as I don't get caught, it's okay. Even in their government, they'll lie as quickly as they tell the truth, and really, they believe it's okay as long as it's not discovered. That's an anti-God mentality.

MOYERS: To be frank, I think that's why so many Americans were shocked to discover that Colonel North, whom as you say is a born-again believer, Christian, admitted that he lied and shredded documents and misled his own peers, as well as Congress and the public. Were you concerned as a Christian by those admissions of Colonel North? You wouldn't approve those things as Christian, would you?

DERSTINE: No, but Christians aren't perfect. They're just forgiven. When a Christian gives his life over to Jesus Christ, his spirit is changed immediately. But his soul is being changed, that's why God saves us right where we are, right in our sin. See, I don't make a big issue of where people are in their life, sinwise.

MOYERS: You don't make a big issue of a Christian not telling the truth?

DERSTINE: Oh, yes, I believe that a Christian when he — when he performs a sin, when he lies and doesn't tell — tell the truth, as Oliver North does, he has to repent. But God is forgiving, God forgives him, God knows the heart of man.

MOYERS: Is God taking sides in this war?

DERSTINE: No. God is for people. God doesn't like to see war, but I believe God uses war. . . .

MOYERS: For what purpose?

DERSTINE: God uses war to — to bring people to him. God is not as interested in our circumstances as he is our heart.

Later in the program Moyers interviewed a Methodist minister, George Baldwin, whose religious faith led him to oppose U.S. support for the Contras. In this segment Baldwin first rejected and then embraced Moyers's characterization of him as "dangerous":

BALDWIN: I grew up in a church where in fact I heard the prophetic word of Jesus preached — the struggle for justice, the living with the poor, the release of the captives. . . . I think one has to—to begin to decide where we cooperate and where we don't, and as far as the Bible is concerned, we're forced [*sic*] with a pretty clear, difficult decision. You cannot serve both money and God.

MOYERS: You're taking this thing pretty far, you know.

BALDWIN: Yes, I am.

MOYERS: That's radical.

BALDWIN: The gospel is revolutionary, in my view. It is radical.

MOYERS: You're a dangerous man, you know that.

BALDWIN: I don't know that.

MOYERS: I mean, if—if your example were followed, multiplied, if your ideas spread, they're subversive to this world.

BALDWIN: They're—I like the way you put that. They're subversive to this world, if we conceive of the whole world as a world defined by the powers that currently are in control. That's right. I want to be a danger to that world.

In his interviews with Derstine and Baldwin, Moyers provides insights into church involvement in Central America, avoiding the traps that space and time constraints set for journalists. Perkins did equally fine work in his 1969 interview with Sirhan Sirhan, who was convicted of the June 1968 murder of Senator Kennedy.

(Sirhan's eligibility for parole remains a public issue. By California law Sirhan has been in jail long enough to require periodic review for parole. In the context of the 1960s Sirhan's act was not considered terrorism, as it surely would be today since he is Jordanian Arab.)

Early in the interview Perkins provided the audience with information and established a rapport with the news source in a nonthreatening fashion. In the middle of the interview Perkins became more questioning and critical. Toward the end he began to ask questions and make observations that would have been counterproductive earlier. As Perkins began to get into the details of the assassination, he asked tougher questions and at times seemed incredulous of Sirhan's answers. Perkins at one point almost apologized for asking a difficult question and then became still tougher in the questioning:

PERKINS: Sirhan, the obvious question is, of course, did you go to the Ambassador Hotel that Sunday to case the place, to plan, to plot, to wait, stake it out, find out where you could shoot him?

SIRHAN: Sir, I know this sounds unbelievable, but I went there just to see Senator Kennedy.

PERKINS: All right, Sirhan, now on the night of the assassination, you said you went to the Ambassador Hotel, had a few drinks and then you said you were too drunk to drive home, didn't you?

SIRHAN: Yes, sir, I did.

Sirhan and Perkins then discussed the assassination and Sirhan's contention that he did not recall a thing until he was at the police station:

PERKINS: You were being held in the middle of the night at a police station with officers all around you and you were handcuffed and it must have occurred to you to ask why am I here.

SIRHAN: I wish I could have. I wish I could have.

PERKINS: But you didn't? . . . Which, of course, makes it look as if you knew why you were there.

Perkins later mentioned Sirhan's notebook, in which before the assassination Sirhan several times had written, "RFK must die":

PERKINS: Well, did you only write them when you were in great fits of anger?

SIRHAN: I must have been, sir, I must have been. They are the writings of a maniac.

PERKINS: They're the writings of Sirhan Sirhan.

Perkins's interview of Sirhan ended with the assassin in tears after he had expressed wishes that Senator Kennedy were still alive and that there would be peace in the Middle East. Perkins again was in a sympathetic role, having asked questions about Sirhan's family.

The interview provided a picture of an assassin who had

changed world history, a slight, befuddled man awaiting transfer to San Quentin Prison. Perkins generally was unobtrusive during the interview, asking questions in an order and demeanor that would provide the audience with insight into the man and the event. A less skilled reporter, one not as sensitive to how the news source was responding and one not as well prepared for the interview, would not have provided the insights that Perkins did.

In addition to the individual reporter's influence, news is shaped by institutional definitions, by efforts to make news rational, and by related pressures to prejudge news and to work for "good" stories.

© Universal Press Syndicate, 1976. Reprinted with permission.

Definitions of news

News-reporting textbooks list the criteria for deciding if an event or issue qualifies as news. A beginning reporting student can recite these criteria quickly, including human interest, timeliness, conflict, proximity, consequence, and prominence. Experienced reporters may not use these terms but instead may offer working definitions, such as "News is what I say it is," "News is what is reported in the papers," "News is something that you know today that you didn't know yesterday."

Journalism scholars enter the arena, too, recognizing significance in even such working definitions as that offered by John Bogart, city editor of the *New York Sun* in the 1890s: "When a dog bites a man, that's not news; when a man bites a dog, that's news." While Bogart's maxim plainly suggests that it is the unusual that makes news, his view also illustrates a turn-of-the-century news emphasis on what people do, instead of on what happens to people. Is that stretching the point? It certainly is, but consider that Bogart's definition came at a time of optimism in science and a time of celebration of the handiwork of man, when the impact of the new technology of the telegraph was really beginning to shape the nature of news by speeding its transmission and demanding tight, crisp writing. Thus, his flippant definition can be used to illustrate a change in journalism that reflected societal changes — faith in people as doers and confidence in experts as news sources.

Whether you take the codified versions of news from text-books, a working reporter's seat-of-the-pants definition, or a professor's effort to find profundity in a comment about canines, it is axiomatic that how news is defined determines what is reported. If a reporter believes that someone is prominent, that person will receive more attention than someone considered less prominent. For despite — or because of — all the seat-of-the-pants and scholarly definitions of news, the criteria listed in textbooks remain good guides, and many news sources know it.

News sources recognize that to use the media to gain attention for themselves or their ideas, it may help to contrive events or otherwise show that their subject matter is newsworthy. They can best do this by spoon-feeding reporters the criteria listed in textbooks: human interest (have the television starlet pose with an exotic pet), timeliness (schedule the press conference or demonstration at a time convenient to deadlines or live broadcasts), conflict (threaten to do something outrageous, as the YIPPIES did time and again in Chicago at the Democratic National Convention in 1968 to keep their antiwar protests in the public eye[7]), proximity (establish a good local tie between the cause and the community), prominence (promote the status of a client by suggesting wide-spread public interest or contriving appearances with people already defined as prominent), and consequence (suggest that many people will be affected or that a proposal is central to the region's economic development).

Conversely, if someone wants to keep an item out of the news media, the argument is that the individual or event is by definition not newsworthy: human interest ("There's nothing new about this; people are divorced every day"), timeliness ("Oh, that happened a month ago. You just found out about it?"), proximity ("I don't think there's any local interest in this"), prominence ("Most of your viewers don't know who I am and could not care less about what happens to me"), and consequence ("This is strictly a family matter; no one else is affected").

News is relative. Events or issues that might be lost in the back pages of Thursday's newspaper—or not even make the broadcast news that day—might receive considerable coverage on a Sunday. That's because government agencies—the source of much news—are closed on weekends and reporters may scramble for something to report.

The timing of announcements, accordingly, can be controlled by news sources to gain more attention or to escape with minimal notice. For example, controversial government reports that have to be released sooner or later may be released during the summer holidays when public attention to the media is relatively low or at a time when the attention of the news media is riveted elsewhere.

Although definitions of the news may not be inscribed on the walls of the nation's newsrooms, the people who want to use the media are well aware of the definitions. At worst the sources have manipulated the media to their advantage; at best they have lessened the reporter's workload by anticipating questions and thereby helping to assure a better-informed news audience.

CHANGES IN THE DEFINITION OF NEWS

Just as definitions of news are not inscribed on newsroom walls for quick reference, neither are they engraved in stone, to carry the metaphor one last step. Definitions do change. Today's news definition of *prominence* differs from that of thirty years ago;

conflict as a news value differs from the definition of ten or fifteen years ago. Those changes generally have been for the good in terms of providing comprehensive news coverage. In recent years *timeliness* has been defined differently, too, but with mixed results.

Prominence and the McCarthy era.   Under long-standing definitions of news, whatever a United States senator said was news, because of his prominence and because statements of such a high-ranking public official were presumed to affect others. U.S. Senator Joseph McCarthy, a Republican from Wisconsin, exploited his virtually unquestioned access to the news media. In the late 1940s and early 1950s he warned of what he called Communist infiltration of government, questioned the loyalty of General George C. Marshall (now widely acknowledged as one of the great Americans in history), ruined careers of lower-echelon public employees, and nurtured the fear, distrust, suspicion, and ill will that are embraced by what is now called the McCarthy era.

The number of Communists McCarthy said he had uncovered in the State Department and elsewhere varied from speech to speech, but discrepancies went unquestioned. News reporters had trouble enough keeping up with his most recent pronouncements and accusations. The existing definitions of news permitted little questioning or interpretation of his charges by reporters.

By the time the McCarthy tumult had run its course, the news media had at least begun to redefine the concept of prominence. The definition was broadened to make acceptable the practice of including in news stories questions about the veracity of a prominent source. Questions could be raised by other sources or by reporters who matched the prominent person's comments against the record or against previous statements. The *Milwaukee Journal* introduced the use of bracketed inserts in stories about McCarthy. The inserts provided information countering the senator's allegations. One 52-inch story included 13 inches of inserts.

For some reporters such changes came too late or were not allowed in their publications. Edwin Bayley, in *Joe McCarthy and the Press*, told how the pressures affected George Reedy, who covered McCarthy for United Press and later became press secretary to Lyndon Johnson. Reedy said his frustration in trying to cope with McCarthy helped influence him to quit newspaper work. "We had to take what McCarthy said at face value. . . . Joe couldn't find a communist in Red Square—he didn't know Karl Marx from Groucho—but he was a United States Senator. . . . It was a shattering experience, and I couldn't stand it."[8]

The news media now are sometimes accused of subjecting all pronouncements of public officials to scrutiny almost to the point of cynicism, but that practice offers a healthier definition of news than the pre–McCarthy era view of prominence.

Conflict, civil unrest, and the news. The concept of conflict as a criterion for news came under analysis in the 1960s and 1970s when editors and others sifted through the ashes in the wake of urban fires and riots and wondered what had gone wrong with America. Editors seemed to agree on at least three points: (1) they had inadequately covered their black communities; (2) they were surprised by the extent of the violence unleashed in their cities; (3) while they might condemn the violence, they recognized there were legitimate social and economic grievances in the United States.

What could the news media do? One suggestion was to lessen the emphasis on conflict as a news criterion. A person calling for the destruction of an entire city was not a more credible or more newsworthy source than one calling for the destruction of a block or of one vacant building. If the riots and civil disturbances merited news coverage, it was reasoned, so did some of the causes of the unrest—discrimination against a sizable portion of the urban population, for example. It was thought that news coverage of the causes of unrest might prevent future riots by helping to recognize, address, and solve problems before they reached the explosive stage. The conflict approach to news coverage had given prime news space and news time to those urging violence and often ignored those working for nonviolent solutions to the nation's problems.

Changing the definitions of news was not a panacea, of

course. Decades later, public officials still mislead the public, and demagogues still find an audience. When their pronouncements are matched against the record, they say the record is in error. Truth has a hard time catching up. Peter Teeley, press secretary to then Vice President George Bush, observed: "You can say anything you want in a [televised] debate, and eighty million people hear it. . . . If reporters then document that a candidate spoke untruthfully, so what? Maybe two hundred people read it, or two thousand or twenty thousand."[9]

Nonetheless, the news media have made modest progress in redefining news when it comes to prominence and conflict. The same cannot be said for changes dealing with timeliness as a criterion for news coverage.

Timeliness, immediacy, and the news.   In retail terms, news has a short shelf life. Nothing is as old as yesterday's news, the saying goes. To keep the product fresh, news agencies try to get information to the audience as soon as possible, and the broadcast media are well suited to instantaneous delivery of a news event or news issue. What could be more timely than presenting news to the audience immediately, as the event unfolds? Certainly there are strengths to such coverage, particularly of sporting events and public ceremonies. But there are drawbacks for news reporters and news sources.

Blind alleys: Much of news reporting is, or should be, akin to library or laboratory research. Before developing the product — a news story — the reporter must sift through much information and inevitably will waste time going down blind alleys. Live news coverage runs the risk of taking the audience down the blind alley with the reporter, sharing information that does not merit attention at all. Howard Rosenberg, media critic for the *Los Angeles Times*, noted such problems in his review of a television special by Geraldo Rivera. Rivera, the swashbuckling television news personality of the 1980s, took his audiences live to a drug arrest. Here's part of Rosenberg's review of the drug escapade:

OK. This is Howard Rosenberg and I'm in front of my TV set watching Geraldo Rivera's "American Vice: The Doping of a Nation." And I'm getting nauseated.
LIVE!
OK, now . . . What you're reading is real. This is reality. This is happening. You're reading this just as I wrote it. Sure, there are muspelled words. Sure, I've made sum mistukes. But it's live. I have no control over it. There's nothing I can do.
I don't know how this review will make Geraldo feel. I mean . . . he's a human being, so I'm concerned. I mean . . . should I be doing this? I mean . . . it feels so strange. But what can I do? This is real. This is happening. And you're reading it.
LIVE!
OK. I think the review, uh, is just about ready. Yes, it's, uh . . . I'm just checking with the copy editors here to see, uh, yes, all right. I'm getting the go ahead. I just hope . . . wait a minute. It's happening and it's real, you see and I have no control . . . [10]

From that introduction Rosenberg moved into his review, noting some of the contradictions between news coverage and the performances by Rivera; he concluded, "The problem has reached crisis proportions. Guard your children. Somehow, America, we must stop the flow of Geraldo Rivera into our homes."

Glibness: Live coverage may give undue weight to the articulate or the glib. Since the first televised presidential debates between candidates John F. Kennedy and Richard M. Nixon in 1960, that format has been heralded as a way to see how candidates react under pressure in face-to-face encounters with rivals. Yet much of the decision making of a president, especially in regard to the most important issues, is carried out in a measured and deliberate fashion. Taking the time to hear proposals and to work out compromises may call for characteristics markedly different from those needed to "win" a television debate. Likewise, such live coverage may give undue attention to established, official, or available sources at the expense of the ill, the infirm, and others whose stories are important to society.

Manipulation: Live coverage makes it easier to manipulate the news media. Generally in live coverage it is the source, not the news reporter, who determines what the audience hears. An articulate news source always prefers live coverage, where he or she speaks directly to the audience, without translation, interpretation, or meddling by the reporter. The reporter and the news process become a mere transmission belt — a role in conflict with the reporter's responsibility to synthesize information from a variety of sources.

Consequently, it is helpful for news reporters, the news audience, and news sources to distinguish between the timeliness of news and the immediacy of news coverage. Timeliness speaks to the topicality and relevance of a news report. There is a danger that the substance of such a report will suffer in the quest for the glitter of immediacy.

The rational nature of news

> Those of us on the outside looking in at government assume that policy is the product of rational decision-making by a handful of men, just as those outside newspapers looking in assume that news is the product of rational decision-making by a handful of men.
>
> —BEN BAGDIKIAN[11]

Of the traditional ingredients of a news story — Who, What, When, Where, Why, How — the most troubling for reporters and sources, and perhaps the most misleading for the audience, is Why. The problem is that in answering the Why, the reporter and the news source may try to explain human behavior and offer easy answers to questions that continue to befuddle psychologists and others in the behavioral sciences.

Nevertheless, the reporter seeks completeness. Why did the president make that comment? Why did the court rule as it did? Why did Congress approve a new weapons system? These are important questions, and the answers may determine the direction of government policy and the course society takes in addressing a social problem. The difficulty for the reporter, however, is that the answer to Why is not always available. Indeed, the person involved in the news story — often the news source — may not know or want to tell why he or she took one action instead of another; yet the reporter offers explanations. Explanations are demanded by editors and news directors, who see holes in stories that lack the answer to Why. After all, such explanations may make the world a bit more understandable and less frightening. It is unsettling to think that forces beyond your control may threaten your safety or lash out at your family without warning and without reason. For the potentially troubled audience the reporter provides explanations.

Consider this hypothetical news story, not unlike those occasionally reported:

> A 16-year-old boy was held by police today on charges that he murdered his parents last night with a shotgun they gave him as a Christmas present. Police said the youth killed his parents [*why?*] because he was not allowed to use the family car after being ticketed for speeding.

So there is the explanation, and most of us read such stories and do not ask any other questions. If you reflect on that example for a moment and still believe the explanation for the double murder, it is likely you will be a rather permissive parent.

Of course, explanations are helpful in news stories, and to caution readers about the explanations, reporters attribute information to news sources. The boy did not kill his parents because they would not let him drive the car; police said that was one explanation. The point remains, however, that the desire for explanations often does shape what is reported.

James McCartney of the Knight-Ridder Newspapers' Washington bureau was city editor of the *Chicago Daily News* when he talked about how irrational events are filtered by rational reporters and served to readers:

> We don't know a lot about most of what we put in the paper . . . we don't know anything . . . we don't know what happened on the west side. Most of what is in the paper comes

from irrational people but becomes rational because it filters through rational reporters and copy editors and maybe a rational editor, if you've got one.[12]

Prejudging newsworthy events

The reporter's work and the role of a news source is sometimes made easier—although not necessarily more accurate and more informative—by knowing just what story the reporter will find or what story the editors expect. Reporting becomes a game of hide-and-seek. The reporter knows the quarry and is not satisfied until it is found.

When an assignment is specific, the hide-and-seek approach is most helpful: "Get the school superintendent's reaction to the court's decision"; "What does the union's executive director think of management's latest offer?" "What's the weather forecast for tomorrow's football game?" Such assignments are handed to reporters routinely, with the understanding that the reporters will have failed if they do not produce the desired information. A reporter knows what is expected, and an assignment is thereby made easier.

On the other hand, the reporter's responsibility to the news source and to the audience for informed and accurate reporting can suffer when the reporter or an editor prejudges a story and knows what will be discovered before the search for information even begins. Just change the wording of the assignments in the preceding paragraph: "Find out when the school district will appeal the case"; "Why won't the union settle now?" "I heard the coach was praying for rain or even a blizzard. Find out why."

Reasons abound for such prejudgment of news, including the incompetence of editors and reporters, but the discussion here is limited to three related problems that sometimes shape the nature of news: labeling; the herd instinct, or pack journalism; and tunnel vision.

LABELING

Ronald Reagan for most of his presidency was called "the great communicator." Physicist Dr. Edward Teller was known as "the father of the H-bomb." Richard Nixon was at various times "Tricky Dick," "the old Nixon," and "the new Nixon." John F. Kennedy's White House was "Camelot." Women's rights activists at one time were "bra burners" and later were "libbers." Opponents of U.S. military intervention abroad are "peaceniks." George Bush, after a distinguished public-service career, battled the label "wimp."

Affixing such labels to individuals, issues, or movements condenses them to manageable size. The labeling process does double duty for the reporter by summarizing in a word or phrase why an individual or issue has become newsworthy and by indicating what the shape of future coverage should be.

Labeling, while saving time and space, may turn a complex human being into a unidimensional cardboard character or convert a complicated social issue into a slogan suitable for a headline or for a TV graphic. Reporters who cover such persons and issues may prejudge what they will find on the basis of what has already been reported and emphasized. Consequently, news stories sometimes only reinforce stereotypes and offer readers or viewers no new insights or observations. Similarly, news sources may be selected according to how well they fit the mold for representatives of an issue, concern, or event.

The women's rights movement early was labeled as an assemblage of "bra burners," and a curious thing happened in the reporting of women's rights rallies. If in some rare instance a brassiere was burned, that was reported. If no brassiere was burned, that would be reported, too—"No bras were burned, however." The news coverage, so practiced in labeling, reinforced the label by reporting its absence, as though that were a surprise and not evidence that the label was inappropriate.

When a label becomes popular, behavior that contradicts the label is viewed as unusual or newsworthy and not as a sign that the label was wrong to begin with or too unidimensional to be helpful.

When Ronald Reagan's presidency was awash in scandal and mismanagement, reporters saw this as a change in behavior from his role as "great communicator," and not as a sign that the label was wrong to begin with. When George Bush raised his voice in a debate of GOP candidates, the *Des Moines Register* noted in a headline, "Bush's attack on press socks 'wimp' label in the eye."

Here is a more whimsical example. Early in the flying saucer phenomenon, the discs were said to be piloted by "little green men." It was routine to include in a news story a report that a witness "didn't see any little green men." The label was reinforced by reporting its absence. Yet one is hard pressed to find any report of a flying saucer or unidentified flying object (UFO) in which a creature associated with the report was said to be green. They are brown, flesh-colored, and nickle-plated, but not green. Perhaps that color became associated with the saucers because no human race has a green complexion.

The labels "pro" and "con" may be deceiving at times, too, when reporters try to simplify coverage of issues by dividing news sources into those two camps and then reporting "both sides" of the issue. Sometimes, of course, there are more than two sides, or the issue may consist of a choice from among several options, none of which is entirely satisfactory. In the abortion controversy those opposing abortion achieved a significant victory by popularizing the label "pro-life," implying that the opposition is against life or "pro-death."

Labels persist because they simplify and organize our environment. It is next to impossible for news reporters and news sources to avoid the use of labels, but the news audience is better served when reporters recognize problems inherent in the labeling process and do not let labels dictate coverage of an event.

THE HERD INSTINCT, OR PACK JOURNALISM

One lesson taught many times in life is that generally speaking it is safer to follow the crowd and not take off on one's own. If you are driving on an interstate highway at night, and vehicles far ahead of you have their brake lights on, you begin to hit your brakes without knowing the cause of the slowdown. A crowded restaurant usually has better food or atmosphere than an empty one, and people react accordingly. At its best, such behavior promises the safety inherent in unified action or reaction and provides a learning experience for neophytes blessed with wise elders. At its worst, the tendency toward conformity may mean that no questions are asked, no new experiences provided, no new paths trodden. If the crowd is going the wrong way, it will continue to do so; there is no self-correcting mechanism for conformists. Habits developed to help ensure physical safety transfer readily to the area of intellectual safety.

In news reporting the herd instinct refers to news coverage defined almost exclusively in terms of what news is being covered. If that sounds circular, it is. The related term *pack journalism* connotes a mob scene in which reporters descend en masse on a person, place, or topic that has been defined as newsworthy, often because it is being covered by other news media. Journalists continually set their watches against one another's. Newspapers use a wire-service story because it must be newsworthy, otherwise the Associated Press would not have transmitted it; the AP later concludes the story must have been newsworthy, otherwise papers would not have used it.

Part of the content of the news carried throughout the nation may be dictated by what is covered by one or two reporters for one or two respected newspapers or broadcast stations and then picked up by the wire services. Reporters for other media then scramble as best they can to put out their version—their own exclusive—of what is being reported by leaders of the herd.

The working day for many reporters begins by reading and viewing what others are covering. Pity the reporter on the campaign trail who does not include in a story—if not in the lead— what the AP or others emphasize. After all, the boss reads and views other news media, too.

Not only is there pressure to report what others are reporting, but a reporter who starts following on her own what she presumes to be a good story might be stopped in her tracks by an editor who asks: "If this is such a good story, then why are we the only ones doing it?" Such doubts weighed on the minds of *Washington Post* editors when they seemed alone in covering Watergate. Seymour Hersh faced that question when he sought publication of his stories on the massacre of Vietnamese civilians by American soldiers at My Lai. James Risser, now at Stanford University, won an unmatched string of reporting prizes—the Pulitzer Prize, the Raymond Clapper Award, the Worth Bingham Award, and the Sigma Delta Chi Award—for his stories of corruption in the grain-exporting trade. Risser, then a reporter for the *Des Moines Register*, talked with federal employees who might have thought reporters to be an endangered species because they had seen so few of them. He was way off on his own, and he was right.

TUNNEL VISION

Webster's *Third New International Dictionary* defines tunnel vision as "a field of vision of 70 percent or less from the straight-ahead position, resulting in elimination of the peripheral field." In regard to reporting, tunnel vision includes such errors as providing little breadth or perspective and narrowing one's perception of what is newsworthy to what has been newsworthy in the past or to what one was looking for in the first place.

Reporters who cover only the intent of legislation and not its potential impact suffer from tunnel vision. So do sportswriters who note only the strengths of the home team, and editors who believe that a new shopping center will be a boon for their city.

Reporters may develop tunnel vision over a period of years of contact with the same news sources. If so, the reporter may see the newsworthy event only from the point of view of the news source, giving little credence to the views of others.

Tunnel vision also relates, of course, to prejudging news and making news rational. In the depth of the farm crisis in Iowa a bankrupt farmer shot and killed his banker and then killed himself—a signal event for dramatizing the anguish and despair of farmers. National news media reported a seeming wave of suicides by farmers as evidence of the farm crisis. It made sense, didn't it?

After several months a state agency issued a report, generally un-noticed by the news media, that suicides by farmers in Iowa were no more frequent during the period of despair than they were in times of rich harvests and prosperity.

Focusing on a new explanation for a continuing phenomenon is not uncommon in news reporting. Unrelated but similar events are suddenly grouped together as evidence of a societal trend or as a measurement of the importance of a news story. This occurs frequently in the reporting of deaths linked with winter storms. For example, a storm is said to have caused a dozen or more deaths across New England, but the death toll often includes victims of traffic accidents and heart attacks that just happened to occur during the storm.

A key to manipulating the news media is simply to know what reporters are looking for. If a news source gives it to them, the source may be able to shape the coverage. Former vice president Spiro T. Agnew knew he was guaranteed wide coverage any time he used an alliterative phrase to characterize the news media or foes of the Nixon administration in the late 1960s and early 1970s. When Agnew or his aides would contrive a phrase like "nattering nabobs of negativism," they knew that reporters would seize on it and perhaps pay less attention to substantive issues. Political writer Jules Witcover quoted an Agnew speech writer:

> This was all fairly conscious. It's amusing, titillating, interest-ing, exciting, to give writers color and bite in speeches. That's how you get attention. . . . The alliteration and the big words captured exactly what we intended. Then the press went over-board on them. After they did that, you just leave it and do something else.[13]

To natter, by the way, is to chat or gripe. A nabob is defined variously as a mogul, a very rich man, or a European who became rich in India. Negativism is the sort of attitude reporters, news sources, and the audience should have toward tunnel vision.

Labeling, the herd instinct, and tunnel vision are not forms of behavior peculiar to news reporters. But such traits are counterproductive when displayed by reporters, who have the responsibility of telling others what is happening in society.

COPING WITH PRESSURES FOR GOOD STORIES

If the prejudgment of news is so risky, why do such practices as we have just described seem to flourish? Partly because there is no record of the potential errors and mistakes routinely recognized and avoided in the news-gathering process; partly because competent reporters and editors have learned to anticipate story developments and to focus quickly on the salient elements of a news story to stay ahead of the competition. To that extent what appears to be prejudging news stories and exercising tunnel vision pays off enough to encourage such practices. But the perception, sensitivity, and occasional good luck of experienced reporters and editors may encourage repetition and imitation with disastrous results.

Unfortunately, reporters sometimes adhere to the facetious advice, "Don't let facts get in the way of a good story." Pressures of time, status, and competition all foster such questionable behavior. Reporting, like other forms of inquiry, is not so much a matter of getting "the facts" or arriving at "the truth" as it is one of reducing the likelihood of error and eliminating the chances that the reporter, the news source, and the audience will be misled to journey hand in hand down the wrong path.

After a story blows up in a reporter's face, it is easy enough to see the warning flags that one should have paid attention to: a news source's assertion or a reporter's assumption that screamed for verification; a comment or quote that should have been a clue to problems with the story; a news source who should have been contacted but was skipped over because the reporter knew what the source was going to say anyway.

Stories that the reporter worries about are not the ones that blow up. Often it is when the reporter is dead sure that the story is "great" that warning bells should sound and the reporter should start looking for those flags. If some information or a news source seems out of sync with the thrust of a great story, it may mean that the story is wrong. For example, one reporter had a great story about a military attaché encouraging more *atomic* aid for Egypt, contrary to U.S. government policies and procedures. But what the attaché had actually encouraged was more *economic* aid. Another reporter had a great story about city government and citizens being so upset with the insensitivity of a federal agency that they had referred to it as *iron ass.* But the agency thus referred to was in fact the Immigration and Naturalization Service, also known as the *INS.*

A third example involved a reporter who was anxious to "keep alive" a story about a serial murderer, who had cut or burned parts of his victims' bodies after he had killed them. When the reporter heard that a body was found with cuts on it, he did not check with the coroner but reported that the murderer had struck again. This "victim," however, had died of natural causes, and the "cuts" were just part of the natural process of decomposing. If nothing else, the reporter's quest for a good story led to an interesting retraction.

Summary

The news that reaches the columns of the newspaper or makes it on the air is not shaped only when the reporter sits down to write the story or to edit the tape. Far from it; the story has been taking shape long before. The news item is already shaped because people see the same event differently or because one person may report an event selectively and differently, depending on the audience.

The nature of the news-gathering process shapes the news at the front end because of pressures of time and space and because of the way news is defined. Definitions of news are not static, and news values such as prominence, conflict, and timeliness have been modified in recent years, not always to the benefit of the news audience.

In trying to answer the question Why, the news media may impose rationality on irrational or bizarre events that defy explanation in light of current knowledge. Some reporters are adept at anticipating news developments, but that can be a hazardous practice when prejudging a news event leads a reporter to focus on information that deals with what was expected to happen instead of what did happen. Contrary to the facetious maxim, reporters *should* let the facts get in the way of a good story.

Telling the news audience what is happening in society is a process fraught with risks. The process can be likened to walking through a minefield. But if the trip is made safely and successfully, it is worth the worry.

③ Interviewing

Why are questions so questionable?

Introduction

SOME ASSUMPTIONS

Two assumptions are central to this chapter: (1) if a reporter, or any person for that matter, prepares for an interview and asks good questions, that reporter is likely to obtain more useful information from a news source than a reporter who does not prepare and who asks poor questions; (2) how a reporter gathers information helps determine what information from a news source reaches the news audience.

If these assumptions are sound — and they seem obvious to the point of being simplistic — why don't reporters prepare, why do they ask poor questions, and why does the news-gathering process often get in the way of good reporting? Much of what follows addresses these issues by looking at the sociology of the question, the strengths and weaknesses of different interview formats, the preparation of the reporter, the competence of news sources, and the nature of the questions asked.

A DEFINITION

For purposes of this discussion, interviewing will be defined as asking questions — an activity pervasive in journalism. To narrow the focus, we will not consider some popular forms of interview — the late-night talk show, the relaxed visit to a celebrity's hideaway, the person-on-the-street reaction to a news event — because they differ markedly from most of the interviewing involving news reporters and their sources.

Perhaps because it follows the popular conception of the interview, one college-level workbook asks, "What devices can a reporter use to put at ease a person he or she is interviewing?" The question is misleading for at least two reasons:

1. The question seems to assume that a person being interviewed can and should be put at ease; but this often is not the case. Many news-gathering situations are tense, uncomfortable, unnatural, hurried, perhaps joyous but more often sad, and being "at ease" would be inconsistent or out of place. News gathering often occurs during times of stress: a political candidate has to defend a welfare proposal; a policeman explains why he did or did not fire his pistol at a fleeing suspect; an elderly person who has never been interviewed by a journalist is asked to describe the impact of inflation on her and her ill husband; stunned witnesses are asked to describe an airplane crash. In much of news gathering, tension comes with the territory.

2. The question implies that there is a certain procedure a reporter can use to put a subject at ease before extracting information: (a) smile politely, (b) introduce yourself, (c) exhibit interest in person and/or subject, (d) make sure source is comfortable, (e) prepare to take notes unobtrusively, (f) ask question: "Was that your kid out playing in the traffic?"

INTERVIEWING AS HARD WORK

There are no surefire gimmicks in interviewing any more than there is one formula for how to write a news story. Interviewing is difficult. The reporter or interviewer is under pressure to (1) understand what the news source is saying, (2) place it in context with what the source has said before or with what the reporter knows to have happened before, (3) think about what question logically follows what the news source is now saying, (4) evaluate the newsworthiness of the material the source is providing, (5) seek to determine consistency in this material by asking the same question in a different way, and (6) do all of this in a manner that will maximize the amount of newsworthy material to be made available to the news audience.

One example of the payoffs yielded by hard work in interviewing is taken from a *CBS Reports* program, "The Case of the Plastic Peril." The reporter, Morton Dean, did an excellent interview of a chemist, in which he asked about the effects of vinyl chloride on employees in the plastics industry:

> DR. IRVING TABERSHAW: Well, I—we've demonstrated that there is a—as favorable a mortality ratio working in the industry as you would expect in any population at work. Secondly, we found that there was an increase in—in cancer. And I can't characterize how much of an increase, because numbers are so small that we cannot really describe them as significant or not. But there is a trend for the workers in the study to have a little more cancer than we would have expected.
>
> DEAN: Dr. Tabershaw, would you work in a plant working with vinyl chloride today?
>
> DR. TABERSHAW: You said "today," Mr. Dean. I think, in the plants that are cleaned up, the plants that are—are properly controlled, I would give serious consideration to working in them.
>
> DEAN: Are there any such plants?
>
> DR. TABERSHAW: I really don't know. But I assume and I presume that plant conditions can be and, I think, are being controlled to the extent of making it safe to work in them.
>
> DEAN: Well, what is that safe level?
>
> DR. TABERSHAW: I wish I knew, Mr. Dean.[1]

This brief exchange is too rare an example of good interviewing. It is interesting not because of any imagined battle between the forces of good (the reporter) and the minions of evil (in this case the vinyl chloride industry) but because Dean was hard at work, asking questions necessary for the viewer to be adequately informed, and because the news source was responsive. The need for the questions about the existence of any "properly controlled" plants and about the safe chemical level for employees becomes obvious once the questions have been asked. Unfortunately, too many reporters and too many viewers would have been satisfied to end the questioning right after Dr. Tabershaw said he would give serious consideration to working in safe vinyl chloride plants.

Examples of needless and poor questions are easier to find. Indeed, the proportion of useful information generated by interviews probably would be doubled if reporters were prohibited from using the word *feel* in any question. Consider a news report in the aftermath of a tornado that struck a small Canadian town in the Province of Quebec, killing two children. They had received the last rites of the Roman Catholic church from the same priest who had baptized them a year or so before. The ABC-TV reporter asked the grieving (zoom in for close-up) priest: "How did it feel?" One of the puzzles of journalism is that reporters continue to ask such questions — questions that produce no useful information for viewers and, worse yet, may delude the audience into thinking they have some information when they have learned nothing that was not apparent before the question was asked. As one might expect, the grief-stricken priest was unable to answer the question, eliminating any lingering doubts viewers might have had as to whether the death of loved ones is pleasant to contemplate.

THE FAR SIDE   By GARY LARSON

The sociology of the question

Concern with questions should be paramount in the reporter's mind because the quality of the questions will help determine how good the news story is. Indeed, from a philosophical perspective the quality of our lives is reflected by the nature of the questions that concern us. That is why, thankfully, most people see the humor in the television ad for the *National Enquirer* that promotes the tabloid as the paper for people with inquiring minds, for people who want to know. Unfortunately, however, there are so many barriers against asking good questions that people who ask them run the risk of becoming social pariahs. The many pressures against asking good questions pose additional obstacles to the reporter working to get worthwhile information from a news source.

Consider the maxims that help socialize children: "Little children should be seen and not heard"; "Ask a silly question and you get a silly answer"; "You can be thought a fool and say nothing or open your mouth and prove it"; "Speak only when spoken to"; "Silence is golden"; "Curiosity killed the cat." Social constraints are such that by the time a child reaches the sixth grade, she has learned that if she asks a question her classmates are likely to think she is merely trying to get the teacher's attention, they will laugh at her if she is supposed to know the answer, and she runs the risk of calling her ignorance to the attention of the teacher, too. In one sixth-grade class the topic of AIDS came up, and that soon led to a discussion about education, television, and condoms. A girl asked, "What are condoms?" and all her classmates laughed. It did not help that at recess other classmates told the girl that they were not sure either what condoms were. Silence is not only golden, it is safe.

QUESTIONS: RISKS, THREATS, AND PRESSURES

Asking a question can be a sign of ignorance—that you have not grasped the point or that you missed what is obvious to everyone else (or at least others have the good sense not to ask the questions). Asking a question singles you out; you have changed the communication patterns and altered whatever relationship existed between you and others involved in the exchange of information. Also, to persist in asking questions, to follow up to get more details from another person, may give you the reputation of badgering people or of not being a good listener.

Asking a question can upset or threaten the information source in other ways. It may suggest to the news source that he or she has not made a point clear. You do not need much experience in education to have encountered a teacher who is exasperated because after three lectures and two assigned readings a student still asks questions about a presumedly closed issue. The question may be threatening because it indicates that, for whatever reason, the teacher did not get the lesson across to the class. Unfortunately, students may soon learn not to ask questions, and the teacher becomes exasperated because after he has presented interesting material no questions are asked.

Questions also can be threatening if they suggest that the news source's point of view on an issue is not the only one, that alternative — even contrary — points of view may be valid. Having made a position clear, a news source may be alarmed that reporters or others still maintain differing opinions.

Sam Donaldson, ABC-TV White House correspondent, tells of circumstances and pressures that discourage questions in his book *Hold on, Mr. President!* He got in trouble with the network hierarchy when he asked President Reagan a question at the dedication of a new ABC News building in Washington. In the opinion of network executives and Reagan's staff, the president was not there to answer questions. The president graciously rescued Donaldson by observing, "Oh, that's all right, that's just the way Sam is." But Donaldson also tells of being miffed when Helen Thomas of United Press International interrupted a cozy chat that Donaldson and others were having with President Carter at a birthday party for a deputy press secretary:

> After the polite hellos, she immediately whipped out her notebook and began asking Carter about the details of his

forthcoming energy program. Carter fled. At first, I was un-
happy that Thomas had ruined the light conversation. But
upon reflection, I realized she was absolutely right to do it.[2]

When Clark Mollenhoff first became a Washington correspondent, his news colleagues tried to socialize him because the
style and content of his questions made them ill at ease. Mollenhoff
was told, "You can't treat a United States senator the way you treat
the Polk County treasurer." Mollenhoff never could figure out why
not, since to him a senator was just as much a public servant as the
county official.

What needs to be uppermost in the reporter's mind is not
whether the questioning process upsets colleagues or news
sources—as undesirable as those effects might be—but whether the
process yields worthwhile information for the news audience. This
is not a question of the ends justifying the means. Rather, it is a
question of principle—reporters and news sources do not hold positions of public trust for their own edification or gratification but
for the benefit of the citizenry. (Nevertheless, interviewers do get in
their own way at times. Italian journalist Oriana Fallaci was so
noted for her interviews that the focus was more often on how she
treated such subjects as Libyan strongman Moammar Khadafy,
Iran's Ayatollah Ruhollah Khomeini, and Secretary of State Henry
Kissinger than on what information the interview yielded. A Fallaci interview can be likened to a bullfight where the concern is
with the style which the torero dispatches toro.)

Syndicated columnist Donald Kaul contrived interviews of
physicist Albert Einstein by persons known sometimes as much for
their interviewing style as for generating worthwhile information.
He wrote of how the young Einstein, having just published his
theory of relativity, might be treated by such journalists as Barbara
Walters, often satirized for her unthreatening questions and her
slight speech impediment: "Dr. Einstein, you were considered a
slow learner as a child. Do you think that spurred you on and
helped you become a success? Do you feel that people who overcome learning disabilities or speech impediments are smarter than

other people?" Or Mike Wallace of *60 Minutes*, known for his confrontational approach: "Oh, come now, doctor. Are you trying to tell us that the path of a beam of light can be bent by simply accelerating it? Well, I have here in my hand a powerful flashlight. We'd be happy to turn off the lights and have you demonstrate your theory, sir."[3]

Textbook illustrations sprinkled with the names of presidents, celebrities, and nationally known reporters are readable and memorable. But pressures against asking good questions are even stronger at county and municipal levels, where reporters and news sources meet not only in a journalistic context but also at Little League games, in church, or at K-Mart. How persistent will a reporter be in questioning a school board member about a controversial issue when the school board member is also the reporter's dentist and some root canal work is scheduled for the next morning?

In discussions of how reporters dissuade colleagues from asking questions and of how news sources may be threatened by questions, an important group is often omitted — the news audience. Concern with the audience helps put the news source–news reporter relationship in the proper perspective. The test then becomes not whether the reporter is liked or disliked and not whether the news source is agreeable or hostile but whether there is information that should be gathered and shared to provide the news audience with perspective on a newsworthy issue or event. Reporters and news sources can still exchange friendly hellos in the aisles of K-Mart if they understand each other's role and responsibility in our system of government. At least that is the ideal.

Some effects of how news is gathered

One might get the impression that once a reporter has the temerity to ask a question the problems are solved and the reporter has the story. Not quite. Remember the second assumption in the introduction to this chapter: how a reporter gathers information also helps shape what ultimately reaches the news audience. This section considers three different ways reporters gather information in interviews: by telephone, by face-to-face conversation, and by press conference. Each method is likely to produce a different story; each may be more suitable for some stories than for others. Each method has certain advantages and disadvantages. Consequently, the news audience may be best served by news gathering that combines the strengths of various methods.

TELEPHONE INTERVIEWS

Professor Eugene Webb of Stanford University, author of two works of value to reporters,[4] despaired of overreliance on the telephone, joking that a book about information-gathering techniques used by reporters would need only two chapters: "The Telephone," and "Everything Else."

If one has specific questions, the use of the telephone cannot be beaten. It provides a fast and inexpensive way to cover so-called routine news: making the rounds of police and fire departments, getting the day's weather forecasts, asking when the city council will meet, or learning the deadline for getting a dog license.

In addition, people nowadays seem to have more time for a telephone call than for meeting with others in person, partly because a phone call is presumed to take less time than a face-to-face meeting. After all, we may think nothing of having someone wait five or ten minutes outside an office, but a wait that long on the telephone is intolerable. Most persons have had the experience of trying to transact some business in person and having their conversations interrupted by phone calls. (In seeking to change flights at an airport, it often is faster to phone the airline than to wait in line to talk face to face with a ticket agent.)

Many reporters, on being told that a news source "cannot see you now," have simply walked down the hall and telephoned the source for the desired information. The more bizarre episodes of this nature involve reporters who telephone a bank and talk with bank robbers while the robbery is in process or who telephone criminals in a house in which the residents are held hostage. No matter how busy a person is, there is time for a "short" phone call.

Another advantage of the telephone is that it permits the reporter to take notes or to tape a comment for broadcast with the source's knowledge but without any distractions. Nor is the news source distracted by the reporter's clothes, breath, or general physical appearance. Furthermore, the impersonal nature of a telephone conversation may allow the reporter to ask more pointed questions than might be asked in person. In a telephone exchange the worst way the news source can immediately respond is to hang up. By telephone second or third calls for additional information are not uncommon, but traipsing back to a news source's office or residence for the second or third time is likely to become unproductive.

On the other hand, a news source can talk on only one telephone at a time. For a reporter anxious to reach a news source, a busy signal is more frustrating than no answer at all. The news source is most likely there but cannot be reached and may be talking to another reporter. Even if the reporter does get through, he or she does not know much about the context of the conversation. Is the news source alone, or are there others in the room listening to and affecting what the source says? Is the news source silently smirking as he gives what over the phone sound like straight-faced answers?

A newspaper reporter was at the Tulare County, California, Sheriff's Office getting information on a drowning from an irascible deputy sheriff, Jim Fluty. As Fluty gave the reporter the written report on the drowning, a telephone call came in from a local radio station; it was a reporter making the rounds of news sources. Fluty's end of the conversation went like this: "Well, it has been pretty quiet. No traffic fatals. . . . No, there haven't been any burglaries . . . No, there haven't been any robberies . . . No, no rapes or murders . . . No, no fires that I know of . . . No, no serious traffic accidents . . . No, no assaults . . . Yep, I guess it has been pretty quiet. Anything else? . . . Good-bye." Jim Fluty smiled. The lesson was not lost on the visiting reporter, nor on the radio station reporter when he learned later about the drowning.

Fluty could, of course, point out that he had been honest in all his responses to the telephone questions.

Whereas specificity is an advantage of using the telephone, time constraints may limit the number of topics a reporter can cover. If an unexpected topic arises or if a reporter wants to pursue new information, there may not be the time to do so over the phone.

A telephone interview lacks the nonverbal communication that might help the reporter interpret the news source's responses. The only nonverbal clue is time — the pauses in a news source's answers. Beyond that, the reporter has not the slightest idea as to the news source's demeanor — no picture of facial expressions, body movements, or hand gestures to pass along to the news audience.

One last disadvantage worth listing is that the news source can terminate the questioning simply by hanging up, accidentally cutting off the reporter, or hurriedly saying, "I'm sorry, I have to go now, good-bye." Any of these is easier than ushering a reporter out the door or walking away.

INTERVIEWS IN PERSON

In person the reporter usually has more time to cover the intended subject as well as new areas that come up during a conversation. The news source's remarks are seen in context; it is more difficult for the news source to terminate the conversation; the news source can make points clearer by drawing charts or pointing out visual evidence. The reporter may develop a better rapport with the source by investing the time and energy needed to see someone in person (indeed, a reporter is well advised to occasionally visit in person those new sources usually contacted by phone). News sources may be reached "live" at a news event far more readily than they can be reached there by phone. Face-to-face interviews carry connotations of the reporter's concern and awareness that are difficult to establish by phone, regardless of whether the phone call is anticipated by the news source or comes as a surprise. Plainly for television or other broadcast purposes in-person interviews are key ingredients of a news package.

The disadvantages of face-to-face interviews are few but important. Perhaps most crucial is that these interviews consume more time and more money—both scarce commodities. Much of the information exchanged in social amenities such as talking about the weather and the family is time-consuming and not newsworthy. Although seeing someone in person can enable a reporter to establish a better rapport, more problems can arise in a face-to-face encounter. The news source may be at best only distracted and at worst antagonized by the reporter's taking notes, by his or her physical appearance and facial expressions, and by a host of other mannerisms beyond the reporter's consciousness. Overreliance on the telephone is poor conditioning for face-to-face encounters. On the phone one can smile, frown, blink, yawn, close one's eyes, or raise one's eyebrows without the news source's ever knowing. These same quirks may have a damning effect on an in-person interview.

Consequently, face-to-face interviews sometimes shed more heat than light, as was the case in the January 25, 1988 confrontation between Vice President George Bush and CBS's Dan Rather, when the newsman, on live television, pressed Bush about his role in efforts to trade weapons for hostages held in Iran. Bush objected that the ground rules of the interview had been violated; Rather disagreed, and the two headed into an exchange that often had both speaking at the same time:

> BUSH: You know what I'm hiding? What I told the President. That's the only thing. And I've answered every question put before me. Now if you have a question . . .
> RATHER: I do have one.
> BUSH: Please.
> RATHER: I have one.
> BUSH: Please. Fire away.
> RATHER: You have said that if you had known this was an arms-for-hostages swap that you would have opposed it. You also said that . . .

BUSH: Exactly.
RATHER: . . . that you did not know.
BUSH: May I answer that.
RATHER: That was not the question, it was a statement . . .
BUSH: It was a statement.
RATHER: Let me ask the question, if I may, first.[5]

And so it went for ten minutes, compounding some of the short-comings of live news coverage with the dynamics of face-to-face interviews.

Similar problems occurred when Louis Rukeyser tried to interview economics commentator Eliot Janeway on the television program *Wall Street Week*. Rukeyser did not get off to a good start when he labeled Janeway "one of America's most persistent forecasters of doom," but Janeway interrupted him even before Rukeyser could say — as he intended to — that Janeway did not like to be called a prophet of doom. From there on the viewer got little more information:

RUKEYSER: Just over four . . . let me just finish the question please. Just over four years ago . . .
JANEWAY: You're not, you're not, you're not asking a question.
RUKEYSER: I will . . .
JANEWAY: You're making a statement . . . You're talking about an interview with me in the *New York Times* by Vartan . . .
RUKEYSER: No, I'm talking about a radio program you and I were on . . . and just over four years ago on this very program, you predicted an imminent market collapse . . .
JANEWAY: Yes.
RUKEYSER: And just the opposite happened.
JANEWAY: Oh. What is . . .
RUKEYSER: And this past winter . . . this past winter . . .
JANEWAY: . . . wait a minute . . . what is true? . . .
RUKEYSER: Could I just ask the question?
JANEWAY: No, you . . . because what you think you are . . .
RUKEYSER: Let me . . .
JANEWAY: . . . is a road company Joe McCarthy . . . he

really was a big league inquisitor compared to your simplistic shabbiness.
RUKEYSER: I'm just quoting your prediction.
JANEWAY: Now slow down.[6]

It is doubtful the Rukeyser-Janeway quarrel could have been avoided even if Louis Rukeyser had had a handy list of things to do to put at ease the person one is interviewing. At the end of the program Rukeyser did acknowledge that "this is the fewest questions we've ever gotten to ask." Such honest assessments often are absent in a third form of interviewing—the press conference.

PRESS CONFERENCES

It is difficult to think of any advantage the press conference provides for the competent news reporter. Use of the press conference by public officials and private entrepreneurs helped give rise to the phrase "pseudo event"—an event contrived to create news coverage where none had been considered warranted.

One value of the news conference by a public official is the symbolic nature of the event, and perhaps this is reason enough to continue the practice. At a press conference in this nation a public official supposedly submits to examination by responding to unsolicited and perhaps antagonistic questions.

A related advantage to the reporter is that the press conference affords an opportunity to get a public official "on the record" with regard to government policies. Statements from a press conference can serve as benchmarks against which subsequent statements and policies are measured. In that regard press conference information may be used as reference points more so than comments reported by a single news medium. Also, when there is a single issue or topic to address, such as a new government program, an airplane crash, or the nomination of a Supreme Court justice, the press conference offers benefits of efficiency in that officials can speak to a number of reporters at once on an issue of public concern and interest. The press conference may be at its best in this almost one-way format.

Generally, however, the press conference format makes it difficult for the reporter to get worthwhile information. At a press conference, particularly a large one, the well-prepared reporter may never get to ask a question—indeed, such a reporter may even be avoided as a troublemaker—and certainly is unlikely to have a chance to ask a follow-up question. Besides, the well-prepared reporter may not want to ask a question, since all that would do is provide information to competing reporters who are content to simply sit, listen, and take notes while others do the work of asking questions.

Most of the advantages in a press conference lie with the news source and not with the news reporter or the news audience. The news source generally decides who asks the questions, determines the length of the answers, can avoid any follow-up questions and rephrase tough questions to his or her liking, and sets the time, place, and duration of the interview. Press conferences televised live for the news audience sometimes only exacerbate the disadvantages for the news reporter, since there is little or no time to challenge, clarify, or place in context material provided by the news source. This was one of the shortcomings of the press conferences of President Reagan. His staff almost routinely had to issue post-conference clarifications or corrections of information that the president had shared with reporters and the news audience. His press conferences served more as a record of misstatements than as a source of information against which government policies could be assessed.

Despite these disadvantages and others inherent in how reporters gather information, the news reporter can help assure that worthwhile information from a news source is shared with the news audience. One way to reduce the likelihood of error is to use multiple forms of interviewing—by telephone, in person, and at press conferences—as well as multiple sources. Common to the success of these approaches, however, are such interrelated ingredients as the preparation of the news reporter, the competence of the news source, and the nature of the questions asked.

Reducing the likelihood of error

PREPARATION

Washington Post reporter and columnist David Broder has earned his reputation as a reporter who does his homework. But the compliment is also an indictment of hundreds, perhaps thousands, of other reporters. What is said to set Broder and similarly skilled reporters apart from others is that the Broders of the world study and prepare before producing their news reports and commentaries. Unfortunately, what does set many reporters apart from less competent ones is that the better reporters care enough about their job — or have the resources available — to do their homework.

In speaking to a conference of Investigative Reporters and Editors (IRE), Wendell Rawls, Jr., the Atlanta correspondent for the *New York Times*, commented on how little reporters know about their subject matter:

> What people tell us really is, at best, only a quarter of what they may know. We really write stories that don't have much depth, gang. . . . You'd be amazed how little we know and how little ever gets into a newspaper. It's no wonder these people [news sources] look at what we write and say, "Jeez, where have these people been? How naive!" So just keep digging and asking — and before you leave always make sure to ask, "Is there anything else I should know?" You might be surprised at what some people will tell you.[7]

The nature of much of news coverage, not just investigative reporting, requires reporters to be well read on contemporary events. Like other professionals and craftsmen, the reporter must keep up to date on journalistic subject matter. The difference for the reporter, of course, is that the subject matter is the human condition. Although that subject is broad to the point of being unwieldy, it offers the advantage that there is little a reporter can read or witness that will not help in covering the news at one time or another.

While news reporters perhaps have been lax in learning to

prepare for interviews, news sources have not been. Recognizing the need to be articulate in broadcast interviews and to adapt comments to the nature of the news medium, many corporations have training programs for company representatives:

> Jack Hilton, who claims his firm has taught the ways of television to executives at 305 of the *Fortune* 500 companies, estimates that businesses now spend up to a quarter of a billion dollars a year to prepare executives to shine under the lights.[8]

There is nothing inherently sinister about such a practice. Indeed, it may be a matter of corporate responsibility to assure that to adequately inform the public about a company's activities, executives are skilled in dealing with the news media. But such training further handicaps the ill-prepared reporter. That's a shame for the news audience, because it doesn't require billions or even thousands of dollars to follow the Boy Scout's motto and "be prepared."

At the most elementary level a reporter can take advantage of a news operation's library, a public library, and current periodicals—academic, professional, and popular journals—for a quick refresher course on topics ranging from sewage treatment to arms control agreements. The axiom here is that some preparation is better than none and that a little preparation is more than many reporters ever have. It is disheartening, for example, to know of the number of news stories and commentaries produced about judicial decisions by news reporters who have not taken the time, or had the time, to read the full text of a court's decision.

Probably no investment pays as big a dividend to a reporter as homework. Many news sources have dedicated a good part of their lives to their vocations or to other areas of interest and activity that they are asked to share with the news audience. Knowledge that the reporter can demonstrate about a news source's area of interest often makes the news source more responsive to questions, if only because news sources have encountered so many other people, including reporters, who have not evidenced the slightest interest in the source's area of expertise.

Preparation can save time. Knowing the news source's background and having even a brief acquaintance with the subject matter, the reporter can move on from there and dwell on questions that will yield newsworthy material rather than simply informing the news audience about the source's age, education, biography, and relatively shallow views.

Even a modest bit of preparation is useful in placing a news source's comments in perspective. On *Meet the Press* a Los Angeles police chief once spoke against gun control legislation. In response to a question from columnist James Kilpatrick, Chief Ed Davis said that only 3 percent of crimes involved handguns, and therefore any effect of gun control laws on crime would be minuscule. Kilpatrick pointed out that the 3 percent figure was misleading because guns were not used in car thefts, larceny, and many other crimes. Kilpatrick added that about 53 percent of the twenty thousand or more homicides in the nation each year involved handguns. It was just a minor exchange of points of view, but the audience got more information thanks to Kilpatrick's preparation than if the police chief's response had passed unclarified.

If a reporter is to interview a person about a subject such as state adoption legislation, strip mining, or fund raising for community charities, then plainly the news source and the news audience are better served if the reporter backgrounds himself on those topics. An interview with a news source for a personality sketch is helped by reading about the news source beforehand, talking with the source's colleagues, coworkers, friends, and critics, as well as reading or viewing material the source has produced. Consider an interview with the late singer and movie star Ethel Waters. In her autobiography, *His Eye Is on the Sparrow*, she disclosed that she was conceived when her mother was raped at knifepoint by Johnny Waters — not exactly the sort of information to be uncovered in a brief interview. Yet this information provided the reporter with an insight into the life of Ethel Waters. Although that bit of background was not used in the news story, it helped set the tone of the story with the lead, "Onetime blues singer Ethel Waters, to put it simply, has more show business experience and more bruises from a cold world than some trios, quartets or orchestras."

The emphasis placed on preparation may seem inconsistent with the suddenness of much news and with the pressures of limited time and personal tension intruding on the reporter and the news source. But that is not the case. Preparation, reading, and critical thinking do not simply help a reporter on one specific assignment. Rather, such practices can become habitual and accretionary, like building blocks. Understanding the legislative process for a bill on adoption helps a reporter understand the process for a bill on strip mining. Having enjoyed in one interview the richness of describing a human being instead of a cardboard caricature, a reporter learns to look for the whole human being in other news stories.

Taking time to prepare when time is available and developing perceptive questions that get to the heart of an issue will pay dividends when time is not available and the reporter is under pressure to structure and explain a fast-developing issue or event for the news audience. That is why, in accredited journalism education programs, students are limited to the number of hours they can take in journalism courses and are required to spend about three-fourths of their undergraduate studies in social science, natural science, and other liberal arts courses that provide insights and nurture analytical skills to reinforce those emphasized in the journalism classroom and the newsroom.

NEWS SOURCES: WHAT DO THEY KNOW?

Being prepared for an interview includes giving some thought to the competence of the news source. The relationships between news reporters and news sources would benefit the news audience more if reporters would frequently ask themselves, What is this news source competent to talk about? What can this person tell the news audience that few others can?

When astronaut Neil Armstrong was about to become the first

person to set foot on the surface of the moon, a television reporter was at the home of Armstrong's parents in Wapakoneta, Ohio, and had the opportunity to interview Mr. and Mrs. Armstrong on network television. What question do you ask the mother and father of the first person to step on the moon? What particular news or insights can they give you?

You might ask, "As Neil is about to step on the moon, what thoughts, what memories of his childhood do you find yourself thinking about?" or "What thoughts of his childhood are most dear to you?" These and related questions would give the Armstrongs an opportunity to respond as only they could. Such questions might also elicit interesting, even moving, answers for the news audience,who would perhaps note that the concerns of the Armstrongs for a son about to step on the moon are similar to those that almost all parents have for their children.

Instead, however, the newsman asked the mother something to this effect: "What do you think the chances are for a successful mission?" The father was asked, "What do you think the Russians are doing up there?" (At that time Russia also had launched a lunar space shot.) The answers from the Armstrongs were understandably awkward and somewhat predictable. They had faith in the engineers and scientists who would send their son to the moon and bring him back, and they were not sure what the Russians were up to, if anything. But that was all. Failure to take advantage of the special competencies of the news source had produced poor, almost useless information, particularly when the parents could have added a poignant moment to the moonshot coverage.

The challenges confronting the reporter are not only to consider what the news source is qualified to comment on but also to seek possible new ways to tap the news source's area of expertise. The latter is particularly important with regard to news sources who have been interviewed so many times that they know what questions will be asked. Their responses are well practiced, automatic, and usually quite quotable. Watching such interviews gives this impression of the news source's mental processes:

Question A. Ah, yes, that calls for response A.1.b. *Whirr. Click. Boing.* And illustration A.1.b(2). *Buzz. Click.* And maybe funny quote A.2. *Buzz. Whirr.* Warning! Information overload for reporter. Move to next question.

Following that approach, the late comedian Jimmy Durante dictated a story to a reporter assigned to interview him: "Okay, kid, here's what you do. You start off with this quote." Durante furnished the quote. Then he dictated the rest of the story to the reporter and said, "And you end with this quote." Again Durante furnished the quote. Letting the reader in on the process, the reporter wrote the story just as Durante had dictated it because the episode offered insights into the man that were difficult to capture in other ways.

Des Moines Register writer Robert Hullihan took his readers along for an assignment in which he was to interview a Miss Pet, *Penthouse* magazine's "Pet of the Year," whose announced goal was "to be the sexiest woman in the world." Hullihan had qualms about the assignment both because of the commercial nature of the woman's visit to the opening of a new stereo store and because of the unabashed use of her as a sex object. He coped well, offering readers these insights into the reporting process:

> Miss Pet turned her big, green eyes upon the reporter. He was ready with his first question: "Tell me of your dreams, your hopes, your heartaches."
> But Miss Pet was too quick; she asked the first question. "Have you ever won a Pulitzer Prize?"
> What a rotten way to start an interview.
> "Well no, but . . . "
> "Oh that's all right," said Miss Pet softly. . . . "I have a certificate of esteem from the Department of Defense," said Miss Pet, her green eyes seeming to urge the reporter toward a question of Pulitzer quality.
> "Er . . . was there a presentation or did they mail it to you?" The reporter heard himself ask the question as though in a troubled dream.
> "They mailed it to me. . . . What kind of question is that?"

(Well, dammit, suppose there had been a formal presentation in Washington. Suppose a congressman had come by to offer her a typing job).

. . . the reporter limped on through the interview until Miss Pet repeated, "I want to be the sexiest woman in the world."

"How will you know when you arrive?" the reporter asked hopelessly. But, suddenly that was it! Out of nowhere! The Pulitzer question! The last-minute comeback!

"Gee, I don't know," Miss Pet said in surprise. "Nobody ever asked me that before. . . . You really are a good reporter."

. . . The reporter strode off firmly toward the peaks of journalism that seemed now to beckon. Now he was legend. Now he was THE MAN WHO ASKED MISS PET A QUESTION SHE HAD NEVER BEEN ASKED BEFORE.[9]

Hullihan's celebration of his reporting accomplishment was facetious, but it is real enough in other instances when a reporter breaks through a new source's well-rehearsed exterior to provide a fresh insight for the news audience. Furthermore, the news source, also often appreciates a fresh approach to a subject the source has been over many times.

Two concluding words of caution regarding the competence of news sources: (1) the reporter should not assume that, because of position or experience, the news source who *should* know *does* know and can provide information; (2) the competence of the news source needs to be linked with news-gathering methods.

As to the first point, Webb and Salancik, in their work on interviewing, summarize four conditions under which the reporter should not give credence to a news source's information:

1. The source may not know the information the reporter wants. This may be the case even if it seems logical that the source should know; for example, the mayor should be expected to know how much the city is spending on street repairs. This condition is made worse by the fact that the source may not know but thinks he does. Use of multiple sources and access to printed records — such

as the city budget, in the case of our example—can help overcome this condition.

2. The source may have the information and want to share it but may lack the verbal skills or the concepts to do so. Children, the mentally retarded, the ill and the infirm, the indigent and the homeless, those abused or ignored by government agencies charged to help them—these and other people have experiences and information to share with the rest of society but may be unable to do so even if asked. (Courtroom testimony of children is suspect for these reasons.) The reporter might be better advised to gather information from such sources through observing than through questioning and might also identify surrogate news sources acquainted with the issues at hand, such as physicians, social workers, and legal advocates.

3. The source may have the desired information but not want to share it or, worse, may lie to avoid sharing information. Again, use of multiple sources can reduce the likelihood of error.

4. The source may be willing to share the information but unable to recall it. In this case some probing by the reporter may be helpful. For example, if a news source is unable to recall when an event happened, except that it was sometime last summer, discussion of summer holidays, part-time employment, family reunions, and other summer activities, or a sequence of photos in a family album, may help narrow the time frame.[10]

Secondly, the relative competence of the news source should determine the news-gathering methods most likely to produce the desired information. Perhaps some information is best obtained by reading articles the source has written; other information may be available in the public record. The priorities of public agencies might be understood better by considering where they spend their money than by listening to what department heads say the priorities are. Certain kinds of information are better obtained by talking to the source's friends or critics, others by merely observing and not asking any questions at all. For example, it is absurd to consider the telephone or the press conference as a way to get needed insights from a source lacking the verbal skills or concepts to share information. Yet reporters' reliance on such methods is one reason that the disenfranchised in society often are disenfranchised in the news media as well.

THE NATURE OF THE QUESTIONS

The introduction by the television newsman made it sound like an interesting news item: "Democrats and Republicans in Congress have accused one another of foot dragging on the issue of . . . " The reporter gave additional information on the failure of Congress to come to grips with an issue and then asked a Democratic party leader, "Do you think the Republicans have been foot dragging on this issue?" A subsequent sequence showed a GOP leader being asked, "Do you think the Democrats have been foot dragging?" As one might safely predict, neither political leader passed up the invitation to accuse the opposition of being derelict. By that time it was clear that what had started out as a news item about lack of congressional action was more a pseudo event created by the reporter's question, since it is not newsworthy that given the chance to assert that the political opposition is at fault, both Democrats and Republicans are likely to do so.

Although it is not always as obvious as it was in this episode, the nature of the question can shape the nature of the answer. A few other observations can safely be made about questions:

1. When people respond to questions, they generally are aware of what the questioner wants to hear. Frequently news sources say what the questioner or audience wants to hear rather than what they think.

2. Questions may be asked in such general terms (Do you support the free-enterprise system? Are you for quality education?) that the respondent can say virtually anything and still be in the ballpark. This makes it difficult to contrast answers from different sources.

3. Questions may direct the respondent to make hypothetical

and unrealistic choices that shed little light on an issue. A candidate's response to a question about support for any new tax increases is likely to provide no useful information about the candidate's fiscal responsibility and budget priorities. In the home, how does a parent handle a question such as "Do you love me or Jenny more?" One of the tricks of language is that because a question can be phrased, it is assumed there is an answer.

The reporter's task is to avoid these and other pitfalls in gathering information from news sources. One helpful approach is to avoid asking questions that call for only a negative or only a positive response. Ask the source questions that provide an opportunity for both or neither. Instead of asking, "What do you see as problems caused by the consolidation of school districts in our county?" a reporter could ask, "What do you see as the arguments for and against consolidation of school districts into one county-wide district?" The first question limits the respondent to a negative answer; the second question calls for both positive and negative comments and is a bit more specific. Some research suggests that respondents are likely to be more candid in their criticisms if they also have the opportunity to say something positive about the topic under discussion.

"Either-or" questions should be avoided if there are a number of alternatives available to the respondent. A narrow question of high school seniors as to whether they will attend college or enter the work force upon graduation does not provide alternative answers for the part-time student, for the person who plans to enter college in a year or two, for someone enlisting in the armed forces, for the student who will drop out before graduation, and for those whose decisions rest on the availability of financial aid.

Webb and Salancik survey methods of interviewing in the social sciences and summarize the ways that reporters can improve the questions they ask:

1. Avoid words with double meanings. Equivocal and vague

wording of questions, emotionally charged terms, and reporters' statements in the guise of questions are of little use in eliciting newsworthy material.

2. Avoid long questions.

3. Specify the time, place, and context you want the respondent to assume. If you want a news source to comment on the general philosophy of government regulation of advertising, say so. On the other hand, if you want the source to comment on a specific measure to ban beer advertising from television, make that clear in your question.

4. Either make explicit all the alternatives the respondent should have in mind when answering the question or make none of them explicit. Do not lead the news source by suggesting a desired answer and not mentioning other alternatives.

5. It often is helpful to ask questions in terms of the respondent's own immediate and recent experience rather than in generalities. Asking parents how awareness of AIDS has affected their concerns about their children will likely yield better information than asking them people what they think about the AIDS epidemic.[11]

Finally, reporters should remember that follow-up questions often are needed and almost always are helpful. In rare instances the rapport established by one good question can have a considerable payoff. Press critic A. J. Liebling told of one such interview:

> One of the best preps I ever did was for a profile of Eddie Arcaro, the jockey. When I interviewed him the first question I asked was, "How many holes longer do you keep your left stirrup than your right?" That started him talking easily and after an hour, during which I had put in about twelve words, he said, "I can see you've been around riders a lot."[12]

Liebling's illustration brings us to the concluding point of this chapter, that of control of the news-gathering process. For the benefit of the news audience it is best for the news reporter to define control of the interview in terms of the information the interview generates. A reporter does not have to worry about losing control of an interview simply because the source is going on and on about a topic. If the news source is providing useful information, the reporter can be considered to be in control, since the interview is producing the desired outcome. On the other hand, an interview in which the reporter has worked his or her way through a list of twenty questions may well have been out of control if it yields little or no useful information.

Summary

An observer or recorder of social and physical phenomena needs to be reminded of the saying "A thing measured is a thing disturbed," which roughly expresses what is known as the Heisenberg effect. Walter Heisenberg, a German nuclear physicist, noted that the instrument used to find a moving electron—a high-intensity beam of light—caused the electron to change its velocity. His finding can be instructive for journalists: "Loosely applied to the already imprecise, unscientific field of journalism, the principle holds that though its full effect is uncertain, the act of covering a news event changes the character of that event."[13] That is the dilemma confronting a news reporter: a newsworthy event or issue cannot be ignored, and yet in paying attention to it the reporter may change its nature or distort a report to the news audience.

The reporter's efforts to learn what is happening are further confounded by pressures against asking questions and against asking people to document their assertions, to explain what they mean, or to consider alternative points of view.

To deal with these problems, to reduce the likelihood of error in what is presented to the news audience, the news reporter needs to understand the advantages and disadvantages of various interview formats. The reporter can maximize the value of the interview by preparing properly, understanding the competence of the news source, and crafting questions carefully.

4 Protecting and promoting news sources

Serving and disserving the news audience

Introduction

Consider the following three perspectives on the role of the news reporter in American society.

— Ben Hecht — reporter, playwright, and novelist — wrote of himself as a young reporter in Chicago in the early 1900s:

> He knew almost nothing. His achievements were nil. He was as void of ambition as an eel is of feathers. He misunderstood himself and the world around him. He thought journalism was some sort of game like stoop-tag. He was a pauper without troubles or problems. He was as in love with life as an ant on a summer blade of grass.[1]

— A broader and more sober view of the place of news reporters in society is offered by Donald McDonald, who was associated for more than twenty-five years with the Center for the Study of Democratic Institutions:

> It is difficult to think of a more important institution in our democratic society than the news media. James Madison put it best when he remarked that "a popular government without popular information is but a prologue to a farce or a tragedy, or perhaps both." Madison added that "a people who mean to be their own governors must arm themselves with the power which knowledge gives. . . ."

Public discourse is a touchstone of democracy. It is inescapably associated with the democratic possibility. Where public discourse is absent, attenuated, or irrelevant, a democratic people are in trouble. And such discourse can only be as informed and intelligent as the journalists who report public affairs.[2]

—Professor William Rivers of Stanford University, a prolific author of journalism textbooks, noted in his book *The Adversaries*:

The stickiest problem in journalism is defining the proper stance of the reporter toward his source.[3]

Ben Hecht's likening of the journalism of his era to a game of stoop-tag is almost as accurate as it is amusing. In the world of journalism depicted by Hecht, most of the time it seemed as though Chicago and New York newsrooms were in the hands of an early-day version of comedians from *Monty Python's Flying Circus*. News sources were foils who existed primarily to enable the reporter to do a more clever job of reporting. A quote or two from the source was proof that the reporter did not make up *everything*.

But the innocence and immaturity that allowed a young nation to indulge reporters such as Ben Hecht was lost during World War I, as Hecht himself noted. [4] The emergence of the United States as a world power, the impact of national propaganda machines and the bloodletting of a world war called for the nation and the press to take themselves more seriously.

Relationships between news reporters and news sources became more complex, as suggested by McDonald's comment. The primary purpose of a news story nowadays is not supposed to be the enhancement of a reporter's ego or the entertainment of an audience. Journalism reviews and various commentators criticize the news media for unethical behavior and inaccuracies in reporting that are child's play in contrast to the shenanigans of Hecht's generation. Today a news story often is handled as though it has explosive potential; in Hecht's time it often was handled like Silly Putty.

The Watergate episode in American history and the resignation of President Nixon symbolize the emergence of a news industry that has been credited with powerful influence, has somewhat adjusted to a high degree of introspection, and has been placed under increasing scrutiny by the audience and government officials. That symbolism holds whether one considers Watergate

DOONESBURY by Garry Trudeau

An early-day Zonker as a latter-day Ben Hecht.

to be a most significant and dramatic accomplishment in the history of news reporting or a textbook example of manipulation of the news media by a news source, in this case the legendary Deep Throat. (The manipulation scenario is plausible since Deep Throat, a government official, might have had to turn to the news media as a last resort. News reporters provided a push when the Watergate investigation had ground to a halt because key figures had been sedated by means of prescription drugs, making polygraph tests useless, and other sources shut up when they learned that investigative officers could not keep information away from the White House.) One way or another the pressures of news coverage helped the constitutional system work and survive.

When Rivers writes of news reporters and public officials as "adversaries" or McDonald discusses the relationship between the news media and a democratic society, their comments reflect changes in society, changes in the news media, and changes in the perception of the roles of reporters and news sources. The stance of the reporter toward the news source—what River's called "the stickiest problem"—is a decidedly contemporary issue. The serving of subpoenas on reporters, the exploitation of the news media by terrorists, the widespread and too frequent use of anonymous sources in news stories, legal actions against the press for libel and invasion of privacy, the disclosure of indiscreet acts of public figures, law enforcement officers masquerading as journalists—all these issues contribute to the debate about reporters' relationships with their news sources. This chapter considers those relationships in two ways: (1) how the reporter *protects* news sources and (2) how the reporter *promotes* news sources. A critic of the press or a fan of alliteration might suggest a third topic, namely, how the press *punishes* or *pillories* news sources. That topic has been touched on in the discussion about consequences of news stories. It will also be considered in chapter 6, but we will not treat vendettas against news sources as a relatively routine or significant journalistic practice, because they are not.

Perhaps what follows will leave one hungering for the halcyon days when a reporter had no troubles and "was as in love with life as an ant on a summer blade of grass." Those days are not gone forever. News gathering continues to be an exciting and enjoyable career; but it is also more complex, partly because society now demands more of reporters, and reporters demand more of themselves. There are no easy answers, but a survey of reporter–news source relationships may suggest what some of the questions are.

Protecting news sources

A reporter might protect a news source by defending the source's credibility and reputation, by keeping the source's identity secret, or by assuring the source access to the news media. A reporter might protect a source for self-serving reasons — to fend off challenges to the reporter's judgment or to respond to criticisms of news stories. As a matter of principle, too, the reporter might protect the news source to help assure that a news medium stands by a story the reporter knows to be accurate. The reporter might also protect the news source at the source's request or for the benefit of the news audience. Of these possibilities protection for the benefit of the news audience is most important. But let us first consider protection for the benefit of the reporter and of the source.

TO AID THE REPORTER

It is a cliché that a reporter often is only as good as the news sources he or she relies on. A reporter certainly is of little use to an employer or to the news audience if the reporter's sources are generally inaccurate, self-serving, misleading, or irrelevant. The way newspapers are read and broadcasts are heard, it usually is the news medium that the audience thinks is in error, not the news source. It is of little solace to a misled reader to be told, "We didn't lie to you; our sources did."

Reporters might protect sources for reasons that include (1) defending the reporter's reputation, (2) being an advocate for a news story, (3) making the reporter's job easier, and (4) avoiding anticipated criticism. In each case the reporter's behavior helps determine what news reaches the audience.

Defending a reputation. Reporters who turn in questionable or controversial stories may be questioned by copy editors, news editors, or news directors as to the veracity of their news sources. Can the news source be trusted? Is the reporter discerning enough to know when a usually reliable source might be misleading? The reporter's assessment of the news source is important because the media can be manipulated to serve the source, and if a story is at all controversial, there are likely to be other "reliable" news sources with other points of view, just as each side in a judicial proceeding produces its own "expert" witnesses. The opinions of contrary news sources will be reported, too, and perhaps given more emphasis by competing media or critics of a news story. If a story has to be modified, clarified, or corrected because a news source was off base, the reporter may be considered less useful for having news sources that cannot be trusted or—even more damning—for not being able to discern that the source was wrong.

Because a reporter has a stake in the reliability of a news source, there may be a temptation to support that source, in the newsroom and in news items, by giving less emphasis to contrary points of view, even when evidence begins to build that in a particular instance the source is wrong. At worst, such an approach puts short-term advantages—maintaining as best one can the reputation of the news medium, the reporter, and the source—ahead of long-term credibility and responsibility to the news audience.

In some instances awareness of ties between a news reporter and a news source will raise questions about a reporter's work. For example, Bob Woodward's coverage of the Central Intelligence Agency for the *Washington Post* was subject to scrutiny after publication of Woodward's book, *Veil: The Secret Wars of the CIA, 1981–1987*. The book drew upon the reporter's access to CIA director William Casey in the last two years of Casey's life. Columnist Murray Kempton suggested that after Casey had established a rapport with Woodward in April 1985,

> the tone of Woodward's CIA stories was thereafter transformed from the doubting to the celebratory. . . . The *Post* would no longer disturb Casey's and Washington's breakfast with some unexpected revelations to his and the CIA's detriment. Casey's friends complain that Woodward exploited him. They can cease to trouble. He knew quite well who was user and who was used.[5]

Kempton's conclusion might be questioned, but his point about the influence of a news source is well taken.

Being an advocate. Protecting a news source is not solely, or even primarily, self-serving behavior for the reporter. In many instances the reporter knows the news source better than anyone else in the newsroom, and it is the reporter to whom editors and news directors first turn if there are questions about the credibility of the source and the accuracy of a news story. The reporter is responsible for assessing source credibility and for advocating news coverage to assure that both the news medium and the news audience are well served. There is a subtle shift here from individual to corporate responsibility. To *not* advocate publishing a news story that the reporter knows to be accurate and relevant may be even more of a sin than to advocate publishing a story to save face.

An editor's decision making becomes more difficult, of course, when contradictory advice is offered by news reporters. In a controversy between city and county governments or between the city manager and the chief of police, an editor may receive conflicting comments from reporters assigned to cover the county government, city government, and the police beat. The fact that such conflicts are predictable (for reasons discussed in chapter 1) does not make the editor's job any easier; nor does a reporter's ego involvement with a story or a news source. Reporters still owe the editor and the audience a candid assessment of the source and story so that the editor can make an informed judgment and shape the story to reduce the likelihood of misleading the news audience.

Making the job easier. In an Iowa story about a woman's murder and the arrest of her husband as a suspect, one reads, "A neighbor, who asked not to be identified, commented: 'They never gave us any trouble. They were a young couple who looked like they were very much in love with each other.' " In an Associated Press story about airborne confrontations of U.S. Navy F-14 jet fighters and Cuban MiG-21s, one reads, "There was no hostile action, said the sources, who asked to remain anonymous." In an AP story about the closing of the *Washington Star*: "A *Star* editor, who asked not to be named and who was at the morning employee meeting, said, 'Everybody's in shock.' " In a wire service story about street violence in Miami: "Two police officers received minor injuries and a 'hostile crowd' gathered briefly when a man was arrested in a downtown park on a narcotics charge, said a police spokesman who asked not to be identified. The spokesman said the crowd dispersed a short time later and the incident was not related to the earlier violence."

One can easily add to this list of anonymous sources by reading most newspapers any day of the week. Richard Scott Mowrer, a news reporter and foreign correspondent for more than forty years, noted:

> Then there's the case of the two unidentified officials, one in Washington, the other in Greece, slugging it out in anonymity. *The* [New York] *Times* of July 4, 1984, reported from Athens: "Unidentified officials of the Reagan administration made the assertion [that Greece was lax in fighting terrorism] in press briefings last week. The Greek official, who asked not to be identified, . . . denied the assertions." Fittingly, the correspondent who filed the dispatch wasn't identified either. The story carried no byline.[6]

Why does a news source need protection for saying that a couple appeared to be in love? Why does an editor, of all people, need protection for saying that the closing of a fine newspaper shocked the staff? Why do police need protection in reporting on what they are doing as public servants? Why does a military person need protection for assuring citizens that a confrontation was non-hostile? Why does a story about Greeks and terrorism turn into a game of blind man's bluff? The answer too frequently is that in all likelihood the reporter was making his job easier.

Facing a reluctant news source, trying to get comments as quickly as possible, or seeking on-the-scene quotes, a reporter extends invitations: "That's okay, we won't use your name." "Well, will you comment if I don't quote you by name?" Michael Gartner, former editor of the *Des Moines Register* and the *Louisville Courier Journal*, told how the use of anonymous sources had sunk to absurdity in a story in the *Wall Street Journal*:

> The story, about an attempt to take over Gillette Company, talked about Delaware corporate law and how it related to the Gillette takeover defense. It turns out that Gillette hasn't availed itself of all the defenses it has under the law. So a *Journal* reporter asked why not. The person who was asked was described only as "one individual familiar with Gillette's thinking." His answer—anonymously in the *Journal*—was, and I quote in full, "No Comment."[7]

To deal with such reporting tactics, *USA Today* prohibited the use of unattributed quotes or allegations. That policy made sense to Gartner, who became president of NBC News in 1988:

> I think that the use of anonymous sources—in all but the most delicate of stories—is the sign of a lazy reporter or a careless editor. I think that the good reporter can get almost anything on the record; I think that the good city editor or copy editor should demand that.[8]

Gartner said that the *Lexington* (Ky.) *Herald Leader* won a Pulitzer Prize in 1985 for its coverage of scandals in the University of Kentucky basketball program partly because its controversial series relied on no anonymous sources—"everything was on the record." There was no evidence that lazy or careless reporters resorted to the use of anonymous sources to make their jobs easier. The news audience was not shortchanged; the credibility of the information could be evaluated in terms of the source.

Avoiding criticism. In other instances a news medium may protect a news source because reporters and editors fear—or have learned—that a news audience will object vigorously to news coverage that is too literal or that violates social norms. Reporters at presidential press conferences generally will not ask questions that are too critical because they have learned that many people in the news audience do not want the presidency treated in a way that to them seems disrespectful.

President Reagan, to defuse charges that he was either lax or lying in saying that he did not remember whether he had been told about a proposal to send weapons to Iran in exchange for American hostages, asked a group of reporters and visiting business people in early 1987, "Everybody who can remember what they were doing on August 8, 1985, raise your hand." Predictably, no one raised a hand, and no one said, "I don't recall offhand, but I know I didn't approve any arms-for-hostages deal." Other senior officials or public figures may carry similar immunity from critical assessments.

The news audience generally does not want its home or peace of mind invaded by "unacceptable" language or detailed descriptions of gross behavior. That point made a lasting impression on editors in Minneapolis when on September 15, 1969, they reported what they thought were newsworthy comments by a person the mayor had appointed to the city's Human Relations Commission:

> "I'm not going to take any bullshit," he said, speaking of intimidation by some blacks and Indians he said has occurred at meetings of the Human Relations Commission and elsewhere. . . . he's not against minority people, he's just against "the 30 or so who are causing all the trouble. . . .98 percent of the colored people in this city are goddamned fine people. I

> talk with colored people a lot," he said, "with the elevator operators, the shoeshiners and in the parking lots, and do you know what they say? They don't buy all this (militant) crap."

What upset readers was not that the human relations commissioner would have such a point of view, but that the *Minneapolis Tribune* would parade such language before them. Also, since the paper's editorial positions frequently opposed the mayor, critics said the paper was biased against the appointment. A staff memo by managing editor Wally Allen in the wake of the dispute noted: "We don't inform readers when we make them angry. We turn them off, no matter how important the story may be. . . . We have too much to do that is important to afford to alienate readers."[9]

Newspaper policy remained consistent with that spirit. In 1988 the policy of the *Star Tribune* of the Twin Cities, successor to the *Minneapolis Tribune*, was:

> A profane or obscene word or phrase may be used only in a direct quote, and only if it is important to the story: that is, if the reader would miss a major part of the flavor or meaning of the story if the word or phrase were left out. If a word or phrase meets these criteria, it must be approved by the night supervisor or managing editor before being published. Where appropriate, we may characterize a person's speech as being laced with expletives without repeating the actual words.

Steve Ronald, a *Star Tribune* editor, commented, "The policy is applied several times a week by either the night supervisor or the managing editor. Gratuitous bad words hit the cutting room floor; major, pertinent ones are run in the paper."[10]

Sensitive handling of language may consider the news source's reaction, too. In rare instances reporters might not publish repeated gaffes by a public official, reasoning that (1) it is simply his style of speaking, (2) at least he is being open in his comments, and (3) if too much fun is made of him, he will just go behind closed doors, and the reporter and news audience will have less access to what is on his mind.

TO AID THE SOURCE

News sources might be protected or supported by a news reporter in a number of ways. Sources might request to review a story before it is published or broadcast; they might request that certain comments not be reported; they might receive unsolicited support from reporters and editors who correct or cover up the sources' misuse of language; and, as already noted, sources might request or be offered anonymity as a condition for sharing information.

Reviewing news stories. It is common in high school and college journalism, and not rare in the professional press, for news sources to request to see a story before it is published or broadcast or, at times, to refuse to comment unless certain assurances are given. Typically news sources say they want to see stories "in the interests of accuracy." There is a distinction, however, between a reporter going back to a source for clarification and a source taking the initiative. In most newsrooms strong peer pressure discourages reporters from complying with requests for prepublication review. Reasons for such pressures include the following:

1. *Competence.* If the news reporter cannot interview people and observe events and report observations faithfully, then perhaps that person should not be a reporter after all. The reporter cannot escape the burden of responsibility for what he or she reports.

2. *Fairness.* Going back to a news source for approval may be inequitable and unfair unless the reporter can do so for most news sources, and this may be impractical or may lend itself to prejudicial behavior by the reporter.

3. *Purpose.* The reporter's purpose is different from the news source's. The reporter's purpose is not to show the news source in the best possible light. Yet this is what the news source may intend in preview of the news story.

4. *Access to information.* In some cases, particularly those involving public agencies or public officials, a request to preview a story is inconsistent with the right that all citizens have of access to

public information. Screening comments may be contrary to what the U.S. Supreme Court saw as the need for "a profound national commitment to the principle that debate on public issues should be uninhibited, robust, and wide-open, and that it may well include vehement, caustic, and sometimes unpleasantly sharp attacks on government and public officials."[11]

5. *Time pressures.* For the most part, news agencies do business *today*, and it seems to border on folly for a supposedly competent reporter to be be delayed while a news source checks a story to make certain it is correct.

The above points do not mean that the reporter should not verify information that he or she is unclear about or may not have understood. The reporter should check frequently and repeatedly with a news source if there is any question about the accuracy of a news item. Such behavior is particularly helpful when the reporter is translating the source's technical jargon — in medicine or economics, for example — into terms familiar to the news audience.

Don't print that. News sources might also request that some comments not be reported, saying the comments are "off the record." Two points should be borne in mind in such instances. Sometimes requests for keeping comments off the record are made at public meetings or in the presence of dozens of other persons. In such cases the comments cannot be off the record, and the source should be so informed. The news source does not have to be a public official but may simply be a person concerned about rezoning in his neighborhood. It may come as a surprise to such a news source that anything he says is grist for the reporter. But the public nature of the comments can be explained to the news source, and he can be given the opportunity to voice his concerns. In any event, the news audience has as much right to the information as those in attendance when the comments were made. Secondly, when a reporter agrees to keep some material off the record, it should be clear to both reporter and news source precisely what information is off the record.

Some reporters never accept any information off the record to avoid ethical problems that may arise if the reporter later gets the information from other sources. (In such a case the reporter might ask herself if she would have recognized the significance of the information had she not already heard it off the record from a prior news source.)

A news source may say something that he or she immediately regrets having uttered. Then the source may request that a reporter ignore the comment. Governor Evan Meacham of Arizona repeatedly fueled calls for his impeachment by uttering insensitive remarks, often inadvertently. After insulting blacks, women, Jews, and others in the preceding weeks and months, Meacham told how Japanese were so excited about the prospect of golfing in Arizona that "their eyes turned round." When the audience groaned, Meacham wondered aloud if he had said anything wrong. In such cases the news media typically report what a source said as well as any statement of apology or regret that follows. The public nature of such comments is one criterion for deciding whether to print them; so is the context and the source's recognition of error. But if a volatile statement is printed, any apology or regret has to be reported, too.

Laundering language. Quotation marks should be treated with respect by the news reporter and the news audience. In what can be considered an unwritten contract between the news reporter and the news audience, quotation marks should guarantee that material enclosed therein is what the source literally said. Unfortunately that is not always the case, because on occasion the reporter is ventriloquist, grammarian, or censor.

The reporter is *ventriloquist* when under the guise of quoting a source he paraphrases the source or uses the quote as a convenient place to impart other information. As to the first point, it often is necessary for a reporter to paraphrase a news source, to translate verbosity and technical jargon into readable or listenable prose. But once that is done, the reporter should not slap quotation marks around the paraphrase just because that is what the source meant to say or could be understood to have said. The second violation of this unwritten contract with the news audience is typified by the following sports-page quotation:

"George Whitcomb, a 6-foot 9-inch tackle, has earned a spot in the starting line-up," the coach said. "The sophomore transfer from the University of Virginia, who sat out last season, earned the starting position and edged out returning lettermen after a fine spring practice and a summer conditioning program in which he reduced his weight from 315 to 285 pounds."

Similar contrived quotes, used to impart additional information or to restructure a news source's comments, are found in other news stories as well. They usually are identifiable because of their awkward structure and because most news sources simply do not talk that way. Although apparently harmless, such mischief with quotation marks understandably makes news sources and some members of the news audience even more skeptical of the news-reporting process. That is a high price to pay for practices that can easily be avoided just by dropping the quotation marks.

The reporter is *grammarian* when a news source's statements are edited to conform to standard English usage but the comments are left within quotation marks or appear as a letter to the editor. An objection to such laundering is that readers and viewers are entitled to know if a news source uses poor English or cannot spell; such information may help put the person's comments in context. True enough. But a newspaper or broadcast station routinely corrects reporters' errors in spelling and language usage as part of the editing process, so that misuse of language does not get in the way of sharing information. If a news medium extends such courtesies to its staff, perhaps it should do so to its news sources as well. Of course, the quotation marks can be dropped when the source's language is changed. And letters-to-the editor sections should point out that letters may be edited.

The role of reporter as grammarian has its risks. For one thing, children and many others do not speak elegantly or write

Churchillian prose, and altering their language changes the mood or tone of a news account. In addition, such changes are unrealistic. By reading newspapers, for example, one would not become aware of how much the phrase "you know" pervaded spoken English in the 1980s. Steve Ronald of the *Star Tribune* in Minneapolis/St. Paul considered the problem and offered this advice:

> Do we directly quote a person speaking bad English, Pidgen, black patois, or dialect of one sort or another? Often, the decision is to paraphrase the statement [and not use quotation marks], chiefly because to use it will reflect badly on the speaker for some of our readers. Occasionally, we'll slightly alter a direct quote to clean up the grammar. . . . [Sometimes] the dialect is appropriate and it runs. As Wally Allen noted [in the case of the human relations commissioner], "A good test is examination of motives. If we have a good and responsible reason for what we do, we need not be ashamed of it nor fear criticism."[12]

In laundering language, the role of the news reporter as *censor* is the most difficult to deal with, because in these instances the direct quotation under scrutiny is not tangential to the news story—it is the whole reason there is a news story. To illustrate the distinction, here are two examples of the reporting of racial epithets—one tangential to the news story, the other constituting the news story.

The *Free Lance-Star* in Fredericksburg, Virginia, one of many well-respected smaller daily newspapers in the nation, reported in April 1987 about racial unrest in Spotsylvania County. The home of a black family "was besieged by gunfire . . . the latest in a series of what appear to be racially motivated attacks." The paper then paraphrased a white neighbor as saying (to quote the news story), "it is the neighborhood's young blacks who are at fault. He claims the blacks started the violence more than two years ago by smashing out car windows." Then the story moves to a direct quote from the white neighbor:

> He says he is not sure how many blacks have been "harassing" the neighborhood. "I do not speak to a one of them. . . . That's not because I'm prejudiced, it's because I don't like niggers."

The direct quote is not the reason for the story. The reasons for the story are the violence experienced by the family of Willie Carter and the activities of the Ku Klux Klan in the area. It is arguable that these events could be reported without the direct quotation about prejudice from the white neighbor. But that quotation speaks volumes. The paper is justified in using it, even if some readers — black and white — and the news source are upset.

The second illustration pertinent here involves a U.S. cabinet official who resigned in 1976 after his comment on black Americans received widespread public attention. (A decade later the general manager of the Los Angeles Dodgers, Al Campanis, and a CBS sports commentator, Jimmy "The Greek" Snyder, would lose their jobs because of insensitive comments made in broadcast interviews about black athletes.) In this instance the comment by Secretary of Agriculture Earl Butz was the sole reason for the news story; the comment had been made privately. The question confronted by the news media was whether to print the obscenity and vulgarism used by Butz in explaining why, in his opinion, the Republican party would not get the black vote. Most papers reported Butz's statements this way:

> I'll tell you why you can't attract coloreds. Because coloreds only want three things. You know what they want? I'll tell you what coloreds want; it's three things: First, a tight (obscenity); second, loose shoes; and third, a warm place to (vulgarism).[13]

This comment was newsworthy regardless of whether Butz made it in a public or a private setting. An Associated Press survey reported that two daily newspapers printed the quote verbatim;[14] two collegiate papers did so as well (at the University of Michigan and the University of Illinois). One newspaper invited adult readers to come in and look at the words for themselves. About fifty readers accepted that invitation from the *Erie* (Pa.) *Morning News*. Newspapers that left the words out justified their decision by saying that regardless of how the audience filled in the blanks, the result could not be worse than what Butz said. Such laundering maintained the focus on the comments of the public official and not on news judgments by the media. Simply reporting that Butz told a racist joke likely would have had less impact on the audience and, in any event, probably would have led to the disclosure of the fuller quote to justify calling the joke racist in the first place.

In the last example there was no good reason to protect the news source. That is not always the case when it comes to requests for anonymity.

Keeping sources confidential. For twenty years or more A. Ernest Fitzgerald has been a textbook example — figuratively and literally — of why some news sources request confidentiality as a condition for providing information to the public. Fitzgerald first came to widespread public notice in 1968 when he told a congressional subcommittee that cost overruns on Air Force development of the C-5A Galaxy jet transport would be about $2 billion. Fitzgerald, a deputy for management systems in the Air Force, was fired a year later and spent the next twelve years in legal battles for reinstatement, which he eventually won in 1982:

> The Air Force, displeased by Fitzgerald's frankness, initially denied the accuracy of his figures. Then they conceded that the contract arrangement had not lived up to its much publicized origins and reluctantly admitted that new agreements were under way and would guarantee Lockheed [the C-5A contractor] substantial profits.[15]

The mentality of government bureaucracy in dealing with people such as Fitzgerald was reflected in a memorandum that surfaced in the Watergate hearings in the summer of 1973. The memo was from Alexander Butterfield, an Air Force colonel and White House aide, to H. R. Haldeman, chief adviser to President Nixon:

> Fitzgerald is no doubt a top-notch cost expert, but he *must* be given very low marks in loyalty; and after all, loyalty is the name of the game. Only a basic no-goodnik would take his official business grievances so far from normal channels. We should let him bleed for a while at least. Any rush to pick him up and put him back on the federal payroll would be tantamount to an admission of earlier wrongdoing on our part.[16]

Fitzgerald came into the public light again in 1987 when he was among the federal officials who refused to comply with a government directive known as Standard Form 189. That document, advanced by the Reagan administration, required government employees to pledge to keep secret not only classified information but also "classifiable" information. Since classifiable information could be defined to include all government information—because almost anything can be classified—Fitzgerald objected to such a sweeping gag order. So did others, and eventually SF 189 was sent back to the drawing board.

Chief Petty Officer Michael Tufariello called attention to $130,000 in suspected overpayments to weekend military reservists at the U.S. Naval Air Station in Dallas in 1984. He was involuntarily hospitalized for psychiatric evaluation, cited for poor work performance, and passed over for promotion. After having served for twenty years in the Navy and having received sixteen medals, Tufariello retired in June 1987. The *Dallas Morning News* quoted Tufariello in its story:

> "None of the money has been recovered, and the officers who knew about the inconsistencies have not been reprimanded. My chances of ever getting promoted were awfully slim. . . . I was given a letter of commendation for doing what was right, but the commendation does nothing for me before I get out." Tufariello . . . said he knew about the incident because he handled the reservists' pay accounts. He said he tried to reach higher-echelon officers but was prohibited from doing so by lower-level officers. . . . A report on May 12 [1987] by the inspector general's office concluded that Tufariello had suffered injustices for documenting the improper payments.[17]

James Olson, a security guard, called attention to what he considered to be lax security procedures at one of the nation's largest power companies, the Quad Cities Nuclear Power Station, near Cordova, Illinois. He was fired three days after he shared his concerns with the FBI, and he said that when he sought other employment, he was told, "You are too honest. How can we trust you?" In an article in the *Des Moines Register* Olson was quoted as saying, "When you do something good for the public, you are not rewarded. . . . I'm sure in this nation some people care, but I don't know who."[18]

Roger Boisjoly was recognized by the American Association for the Advancement of Science for his "whistle blowing" in helping reveal the cause of the explosion of the space shuttle Challenger. He received the association's Freedom and Responsibility Award. But Boisjoly has filed a billion-dollar lawsuit against his former employer, Morton Thiokol, for "post-traumatic stress" suffered in the wake of his disclosures.[19]

Fitzgerald, Tufariello, Olson, and Boisjoly did not request confidentiality nor seek anonymity, but their cases suggest why others do. Employees often are the sources of information about misdeeds, errors, and corruption of high-ranking officials, public and private. Because of the employees' vulnerability—perceived threats to job security and promotion—such people may request anonymity when talking with reporters. In criminal matters news sources may fear for their physical safety if they are identified. Sharing information that the public should know if it is to govern wisely can be risky, even though in the United States the public is sovereign.

Nevertheless, before granting a news source anonymity, the news reporter needs to consider: Is the information available elsewhere? Is it reasonable to persuade the news source to be identified? Is the news source seeking anonymity to avoid retribution or to avoid responsibility? Is the information of such a crucial nature to the story and to the news audience that the reporter would be irresponsible *not* to provide anonymity?

TO AID THE NEWS AUDIENCE

Much of the history of twentieth century American journalism is being written in the courtrooms, as judges, prosecuting attorneys, and lawyers consider to what extent the First Amendment and state "shield laws" grant news reporters the privilege of not divulging information sought by grand juries, police, or parties in civil litigation. The issue is simple and yet profound. The system of government in the United States requires an informed electorate capable of self-government. In the process of providing information to the public, news reporters at times promise a news source that the source's identity will not be revealed or that some information learned in the news-gathering process will not be divulged. The orientation toward protecting the news source is inextricably linked with benefiting the public.

To serve the news audience, reporters generally have used three defenses to protect the anonymity of news sources and the confidentiality of information. (1) They argue that the First Amendment guarantee of freedom of the press and similar guarantees in state constitutions protect the news-gathering process from judicial intrusion. (2) Shield laws and judicial decisions in most states now provide some protection to reporters and their sources. Before a court can order a news reporter to identify a source or divulge information, it must apply a test that includes these questions: Is the information sought necessary or critical to the case at issue? Have all other reasonable means to get the information from other sources been exhausted? Is it clear that the request is not frivolous? If a court finds that the information sought goes to the heart of a legal proceeding, that it is not available from other sources, and that the request is not a frivolous one—only then can it order a reporter to identify a news source or share "confidential" information.[20] (3) Reporters may be willing to go to jail as an act of civil disobedience rather than disclose news sources.

News sources sometimes need the assurance that a news reporter is willing to go to jail or that the law will protect a pledge of confidentiality, as the episodes involving Fitzgerald, Tufariello, Olson, and Boisjoly suggest. Also, without a reporter's privilege to keep news sources and related information confidential, the views of many dissidents and the so-called disenfranchised might not reach the public. The news media can provide a forum for those whose political views and activities virtually preclude them from holding public office or having access to other public forums such as appointed committees and civic organizations. The reasoning here is that it is important for all segments of society to know what others are thinking, and that a sizable portion of society is likely to have an incomplete picture of an issue if it is not made aware of the views of minority and dissident groups. To deny such groups access to the news media may only foment violence. That point was raised in 1800 by Tunis Wortman, a New York lawyer, and paraphrased by historian Leonard Levy:

> Men whose only guilt consists of credulity, zeal, prejudice, mistaken opinion, or "imbecility of understanding" are victimized by prosecutions, with the result that the free formation of public opinion is destroyed and a pernicious silence creeps over society. . . . Indeed, by damming up discontent and removing the possibility of its verbal expression, prosecution makes a resort to violence more likely.[21]

The shield law issue — providing legal protection for reporters who want to keep news sources confidential — is not as clear-cut as much of the preceding discussion might suggest. There is no unanimity among news reporters as to whether shield laws are necessary and if so, whether they should be enacted by legislatures or the courts. Those who argue against such protection point out that journalists typically have opposed special privileges for any class of society. They also fear that unscrupulous reporters might abuse shield laws by making unsubstantiated charges and then claiming a right to protect a nonexistent source. Critics also scoff at a call for legal machinery to provide confidentiality in a few warranted and rare cases when reporters grant anonymity so routinely.

Nor do all journalists applaud when a state passes a shield law. They reason that if a legislature passes such a law, it can amend it or repeal it just as easily. They suggest that the First

Amendment, a journalist's willingness to go to jail, and trust between news reporters and news sources are sufficient—if not better—guarantees of anonymity and confidentiality of information.

Experience with a California shield law supports this view. The California law provided that news reporters "cannot be found in contempt by a court, the legislature, or any administrative body for refusing to disclose the source of *any information* for publication and published in a newspaper" (emphasis added). That seems explicit. Yet the managing editor and three reporters of the *Fresno Bee* spent two weeks in jail for refusing to tell a judge their source of information about grant jury testimony on alleged bribery involving a city official. The four had acknowledged that the information was furnished by someone not bound by an order issued by Judge Denver Peckinpah not to discuss the case with the news media. Still, the jail sentences resulted because the judge said the legislature could not tell him how to run his courtroom, and the state supreme court declined to hear an appeal.[22]

Since shield law legislation and court interpretations of the First Amendment will change through the years, what relatively stable guidelines exist for the reporter in serving the news audience and respecting a news source's request for anonymity?

1. Pledges of confidentiality should not be made lightly. One should not readily dismiss the link between what is said and who says it. The credibility of information should depend upon the source more than any other single factor. News organizations often require reporters to inform editors or news directors of pledges of anonymity to assure that the news organization is willing to fight whatever legal battles might ensue. Also, some news organizations require second and third independent sources of information to verify the original source's story. In the quest for verification, however, reporters and editors must be equally sensitive to contradictory sources. The original source's information is hardly verified if three additional sources support it but others contradict it.

2. The duty of all citizens to testify in court is deeply rooted in our system of justice, as is the right of the accused to confront

those making charges against them. No court or grand jury will waive these duties and rights merely to satisfy ill-founded or whimsical requests by reporters to keep sources of information confidential.

3. To provide access to the news media for all segments of society, reporters may on occasion promise news sources that their identities will be kept secret and that certain information will not be disclosed. When such guarantees are made, the reporter and the reporter's employer accept the consequences. Columnist Jack Anderson dropped a $22 million lawsuit against former president Richard Nixon and top officials of the Nixon administration rather than disclose sources of news stories involved in the litigation. U.S. District Court Judge Gerhard A. Gesell had said, "There is substantial indication that plaintiff can prove acts of official harassment . . . to interfere with his work as a newspaperman," but the trial could not proceed unless Anderson revealed "the names of all his relevant sources." Anderson did not, the trial did not proceed.

Conversely, in the summer of 1987 editors at *Newsweek* felt that circumstances permitted—if they did not require—the magazine to identify Lt. Col. Oliver North as the confidential source of information for a story related to the October 1985 hijacking of the cruise ship the *Achille Lauro*.[23] *Newsweek* did so after North, in testimony before the Iran-Contra hearings, said that deception of Congress was justified because representatives and senators often leaked sensitive information, as they did in the *Achille Lauro* case. Such duplicity had to be disclosed, *Newsweek* decided, although its Washington bureau and others, including investigative reporter Seymour Hersh, said that *Newsweek* had to honor its commitment of confidentiality, even if North was lying on national television.[24] The episode illustrates some of the sticky situations that can arise when confidentiality is granted.

4. The news reporter or the news medium does not set all the rules on confidentiality and cannot anticipate when the issue will arise. A reporter might be ordered by a court to disclose a source, or a television station might be subpoenaed for outtakes (unbroadcast videotape) in cases where no confidentiality was promised. For

example, in a civil suit WHO-TV in Des Moines, Iowa, was asked to provide its outtakes of a public suicide. For several hours an 18-year-old man had held police at bay while he played Russian roulette with a high-powered handgun. After several spins of the cylinder, he lost. The grieving family filed suit against the city and contended that the WHO-TV outtakes would show that there were opportunities for police to have rushed and disarmed the young man before he killed himself. WHO-TV fought the family's subpoena as a matter of principle and to avoid setting a precedent, arguing that it is a news agency and does not gather information for the benefit of parties in litigation. The Iowa Supreme Court returned the case to a lower court, holding that the family's request did not address the test of whether the subpoenaed information was available elsewhere or went to the heart of the issue.

Furthermore, in almost any litigation one side or the other can benefit from delay. Consequently, an attorney might subpoena information from a news organization — even knowing that the subpoena will be fought and perhaps found unwarranted — because a long shot might pay off, because the delay will work to the client's advantage, or because the attorney must explore every possible avenue in the case. All the more reason for news reporters and their editors and news directors to understand the principles involved in sharing unpublished or unbroadcast information.

5. To protect themselves, news sources need to recognize that a reporter's pledge of confidentiality may need to be approved by a supervising editor, a company lawyer, or others. For the news source the issue involves confidence and trust in the news reporter and recognition that the information to be shared is so important to the public that the news source may risk the consequences of eventually being identified, since the pledge of confidentiality is not ironclad. Such an approach might lead a news source to the appropriate conclusion that he or she is willing to be identified from the outset.

6. Not all requests for anonymity need to be studied under a legal microscope. Reading a newspaper, viewing television, or listening to the radio daily will demonstrate that reporters routinely

grant anonymity in reporting a wide range of items, from talk in a baseball locker room to conversations in a U.S. Senate cloakroom. Use of an anonymous source should be conditioned on a three-part test: How important is the information to the news audience? Is it likely the source will suffer solely because he or she is linked to the information? Is the desired information available from other sources, including public records, where anonymity will not be an issue? Often reporters and news sources get caught up in gamesmanship or in personal priorities. Refocusing on benefits to the news audience is a helpful way to crystalize thinking about requesting or granting confidentiality.

Promoting news sources

Sociologists Paul Lazarsfeld and Robert Merton introduced the concept of "status conferral" in a classic discussion of media effects. They observed:

> The mass media confer status. . . . Enhanced status accrues to those who merely receive attention in the media, quite apart from any editorial support. The mass media bestow prestige and enhance the authority of individuals and groups by legitimizing their status. Recognition by the press . . . testifies that one has arrived.[25]

Lazarsfeld and Merton suggested that the course of public debate on social issues and the emergence of spokespersons and leaders on those issues may depend in large part on the media's choice of news sources. (Equally important, as recognized by the news media in more recent years, is that the nature of the debate also is affected when the news media ignore potential news sources—a concern of the next chapter.)

Promoting news sources—enhancing or reinforcing their reputation, power, or prestige—is inherent in much of news reporting.

A cyclical process. Because a news source once is quoted speaking out on a certain issue, he or she gains increased recognition and status. The news source is sought by reporters for comment when the issue arises again. A reporter turning in a story without a quote from a person who has been quoted on the issue before may be asked to get a comment from the established source, too. One can almost hear the editor: "We can't have a story on ＿＿＿＿＿＿＿ without a comment from ＿＿＿＿＿＿＿＿."

Well-established sources may also be sought for comment on tangential issues. And a source that has really "arrived" may be asked for comment on issues and events that he or she knows nothing about — witness the attention paid to any celebrity's or politician's views on the Superbowl, the World Series, child rearing, and other sundry topics. In these cases who the source is for outweighs what the information is. In addition, a reporter's reputation is enhanced because he or she is able to get comment from such a reputable source, even if on this particular topic the source speaks gibberish.

Rolodex journalism.   Public affairs and news programming in the broadcast media have given rise to the term "Rolodex journalism," which suggests a format in which the news reporter or producer has a stable of news sources and spins through the listing of regular sources to see who is available for comment tonight, who can be counted on to provide a certain point of view. Another resource often used by reporters is the newsroom library, which includes information from previous issues of the newspaper and tapes from previous shows. A reporter assigned to cover an event or issue need only check the files to learn the background and to find out who the recognized sources are.

Self-protection.   In lawsuits for libel or invasion of privacy, a court will consider how responsible a news organization was in its coverage — whether the coverage was reckless and irresponsible or was generally consistent with accepted journalistic practices. Plainly, in such instances the news organization's case is enhanced if the story in question included, or was based on, comments from established, recognized news sources, such as public officials or others with expertise in the subject. In its own self-interest a news organization may be well advised to include established sources in potentially litigious stories. That practice becomes another vehicle for promoting a news source. This approach may work to the disadvantage of members of minority groups and dissidents whose credentials might not impress a court as warranting the attention of the news media.

Earned status. An advertisement for an investment firm suggested that the company made money the old fashioned way: they earned it. Similarly, a news source might become prominent – not in a sinister or contrived fashion – because she or he earned it. Inherent in any promotion of a news source is the fact that some news sources are routinely relied on because of their position or expertise. Government officials have status as news sources because of their responsibilities to the public. Reporters turn to established sources not only because they have been utilized in the past but also because these sources have been found to be articulate, credible, and reliable. To that extent the promoting and reinforcement of news sources is inherent in the news process.

If there is one key adjective that earns a news source status in a reporter's eyes, it is *helpful.* A potential news source who is perceived as helpful to the reporter and to the news audience will get far more attention than one who is perceived as self-serving. The best way for a person or an institution to get recognition in the news media is to help the reporter understand an issue or event and its relevance to the news audience.

Summary

Often the news media are accused of biased news coverage, of plainly – in the critic's eye – favoring one news source or one issue over another. Newsrooms often are intrigued, amused, or puzzled that readers and viewers divine their coverage of the news as complicated, conspiratorial plots on behalf of one side or another. The discussion on protecting and promoting news sources should at least suggest that the subtleties and complexities of the reporting process may do more to shape what is reported than any heavy-handed conspiracy.

News sources may be protected by the news reporter in a variety of ways, to the benefit of the reporter and of the source. But that protection and those benefits rest on the assumption that the news audience is the ultimate benefactor. If the news audience is misled so that a reporter's ego can be assuaged, or if the news audience is shortchanged crucial information to protect or promote a news source, then the reporting process fails. Focusing on benefits to the news audience can help crystalize issues for the reporter and facilitate decision making.

Anonymity is granted too often and too easily. Before putting a cloak over a news source, the reporter needs to consider such questions as whether the information is available elsewhere, whether it is reasonable to persuade the news source to forgo confidentiality, and whether the news source is seeking anonymity to avoid retribution or responsibility. A final test is whether the information is so crucial that a reporter would be irresponsible not to provide anonymity.

Although much in the reporting process works to the advantage of established news sources and the status quo, one value of the use of anonymous sources is that the practice may provide minority and dissident groups access to the news media.

5 Conventional and nonconventional news sources

Different sources, common problems

Introduction

News from both conventional and nonconventional sources is needed to complete the societal pictures that the news media compose for the public.

Conventional news sources are considered in operational terms: the way the news media gather most of their information. That means through and from beats or governmental offices; public relations or promotional sources; attendance at newsworthy events; and use of public records.

Some relatively newer or less frequently used approaches to news gathering include (1) so-called precision journalism, (2) contact with minority groups and the disenfranchised, and (3) responses to the bizarre role of terrorist groups, significant not because of the amount of news they generate but because of the questions they raise about the news-reporting process. For the sake of contrast and organization these sources are called *nonconventional*, despite the fact that some have been around for a long time.

Discussions in this book about the power of the press, interviewing, the pitfalls awaiting the reporter, and protecting and promoting news sources are relevant to both conventional and nonconventional news sources. Changing the status of the news source does not necessarily reduce the likelihood of biased, incomplete, or inaccurate reporting.

Differences between conventional and nonconventional news sources are better understood in terms of (1) the frequency with which they are used by news reporters, (2) the costs of news coverage (since nonconventional sources may require more time and since related costs are not always built into newsroom budgets), and (3) the questions of news judgment that arise. Because nonconventional sources may constitute seldom-explored territory, many news-gathering issues connected with them have not been widely discussed or been turned into routine, as they have with news coverage of school boards, sports, or city government.

Conventional news sources

BEATS

Listing typical news beats is akin to saying the words "mom" and "apple pie." A list of beats is a recitation of social and political institutions generally revered or respected for their roles in society: the courthouse, city hall, school board, police and fire departments, business, real estate, sports, fraternal organizations, the legislature, religion, and others, depending upon local interests, industries, and government agencies. Not all these beats receive the same amount of news coverage, of course, but as sources they are turned to on such a routine basis that typically one or two reporters assigned to them carry the responsibility for generating most of the news. Also, at most news operations a reporter will be responsible for more than one such beat.

Convenient and necessary. Even a cursory reading of the list of beats should suggest why it is convenient and perhaps necessary to structure so much of news coverage in this fashion. Beats are predictable and continuing sources of news in terms of the effects they have upon the public and the services they are supposed to provide. The day-to-day occurrences on beats are well suited to satisfying such news criteria as proximity, prominence, timeliness, consequence, human interest, and occasionally even conflict.

News from a beat generally is continuing and interrelated: action taken in May is related to action taken in December; Tuesday's comments are related to Thursday's arguments. Consequently, it is useful to have the same reporter covering a beat over a period of time. From the standpoint of accounting, the news medium gets a better return on the reporter's salary (less time is spent learning the ropes and more time reporting). The beat system lends itself well to newsroom organization and to a division of labor according to the competence, interests, and abilities of the reporters. In addition, the audience is more likely to benefit from informed coverage that is placed in perspective of the news source's past actions and future options.

At its best the beat system provides members of the news audience with informed reporting of issues and events likely to affect their lives, from an increase in taxes to public services financed by those taxes, and memorializes significant events in the lives of citizens, from births to deaths.

Some shortcomings.   Weaknesses of the beat system are fewer but spring from the very source of its strengths: the assumption of news worthiness and continuing coverage by the same reporter. News coverage might be given to a beat for the same reason that a person climbs a mountain, "because it's there," and not because every action on the beat is newsworthy. The value of continuing coverage is jeopardized by turnover in newsroom staffs. Given the mobility of news reporters, particularly in the broadcast industry, conventional news sources may have to "educate" a new reporter every several months or so. In this context it is difficult to sustain well-informed news reporting. Long-term relationships pose problems too. Familiarity with the beat and the news sources, sympathy with a source's problems, and a sense of responsibility for the success of the source's programs may become overriding concerns—to the point that the reporter confuses them with responsibility to the news audience. Such concern is an understandable and predictable result of prolonged and thoughtful communication between a news source and a news reporter.

Problems arising from this relationship become apparent in several ways:

—When a news medium is working on a controversial story that may put a regular news source in an unfavorable light, a reporter other than the one who routinely covers the source may draw the assignment. The reasoning is that the news medium does not want to jeopardize the long-term relationship between the beat reporter and the news source.

—When conventional news sources differ in their points of view, the differences may be reflected in the newsroom by the reporters who cover the beats involved. As noted in the preceding chapter, an editor trying to understand what is happening between the chief of police and the city manager is likely to get differing accounts from the police reporter and the city hall reporter.

—When a beat reporter is on vacation or ill and a replacement reporter moves in for even a week or two, news coverage may take curious and humorous turns. School board or city council members accustomed to a friendly and informal relationship with a beat reporter may be astonished and embarrassed when they read the coverage of their meeting and learn that the interim reporter has written about what the beat reporter had ignored. The reader or viewer gets a markedly different view of an agency because of changes or variations in the beat system.

In addition, the substitute reporter may have a more difficult time obtaining information because of loyalty or trust the news source has established with the regular reporter. Police, for example, may have confidence that the regular reporter will not disclose information that might jeopardize an investigation or an arrest, even if that information is part of the public record, but they are leery of any replacement. The news source might save some helpful background information until the regular reporter returns, recognizing that there is no need to establish a measure of equity with the short-term replacement.

These examples all illustrate a common point: relationships between reporters and news sources who see one another almost daily will differ from relationships between reporters and news sources who meet or who talk on the telephone only once. The reporter in the former situation, by almost all that is known about human behavior, will seek at least a cordial relationship with the continuing news source, and that is likely to affect the nature of the news that reaches the public.

Some remedies. Problems inherent in the system can be offset internally by rotating reporters among beats, which will also help develop a well-rounded staff. Externally, some of the risks of beat coverage — as posed by the newsroom — are offset because conventional news sources do not rely solely on the press and do not operate in a vacuum. Public agencies, as well as nonprofit organizations, compete for public support and for their share of the tax dollar and charity monies. Thus if a newspaper neglects an agency, it will find other ways to get its message across. If a competitor gets coverage that is too favorable or is inaccurate, a competing agency is likely to call that to the attention of another reporter or news organization. Although far from perfect, the process can help assure that the news audience is informed — perhaps later than sooner, however.

Concerns that the beat system simply reinforces the status quo are legitimate but can be offset by use of nonconventional sources. Long-standing social institutions, however, also have concerns about the adequacy of the news coverage they receive. For example, given the role of religion in American life, it would be logical to consider churches as primary and plentiful conventional news sources. But Cal Thomas, who worked for a religious organization and also was a broadcast newsman, lamented the shallowness of the coverage of religious news:

> The problem is that many of us in the news business have traded our natural skepticism for cynicism when it comes to spiritual things.
>
> We have dealt in stereotypes, or with the excesses of those who profess religious commitment, or we have tried to ignore the subject altogether by dumping everything "religious" (except great controversies) into the ghetto of the religion page.

> As the religion editor of the *New York Times*, Kenneth Briggs, once observed, "Most editors are working off a negative Sunday school experience," and that is why they turn a blind eye in the direction of anything remotely resembling a story with a spiritual dimension.[1]

To offset such news coverage problems, perceived or real, many sources of conventional news employ public relations or public information persons to help get their stories across to the public.

PUBLIC RELATIONS AND PROMOTIONAL PERSONNEL

Mention of public relations (PR) conjures two mental images for veteran reporters: the news release and the wastebasket. Or so they would have you believe. For many journalists the working day begins by going through mail received from news sources and aspiring news sources. While much of that mail contains news releases that are wastebasket bound, public relations and promotional personnel provide a subsidy of information to the news reporter and the news audience. In recent years that subsidy has become more appreciated in newsrooms, moving from grudging acceptance to recognition that the public relations information subsidy helps the news reporter do a more thorough job of informing the news audience.

Professor Judy VanSlyke Turk of the University of Oklahoma assessed the influence of public relations activities on news media content. She examined how eight daily newspapers in Louisiana used information generated by six state agencies (Agriculture, Commerce and Industry, Justice, Public Safety, Revenue and Taxation, and Secretary of State).[2] Over an eight-week period the six state agencies provided 444 information subsidies to the newspapers. The larger categories of subsidies were 215 news releases, 92 telephone calls from agencies to the newspapers, and 71 responses to newspaper phone calls. Other forms of subsidies included agency documents, press conferences, and face-to-face meetings. Public information officers at the state agencies batted a little better than .500 in getting the media to use these subsidies:

> The newspapers used 225, or 51 percent, of the 444 information subsidies they received from PIOs for the six state agencies. . . . Use of these 225 handouts resulted in the publication of 183 separate news stories, or 48 percent of all 383 stories the newspapers published about the six agencies during the eight-week period.[3]

The study, of course, does not reveal even the tip of the iceberg in terms of subsidies provided to the news media. It is likely that information provided by representatives of the weather service or of a local funeral home are used almost 100 percent of the time in weather reports or obituaries. On the other hand, information from national organizations with no local ties is hardly used at all. But even if the public relations information does not reach the news audience, it does provide potential background for the news reporter.

Given this reciprocal relationship between the source and the reporter, why is there antipathy between them at times? Many reporters who have been aided by public relations and publicity personnel carry embarrassing scars or bad memories because of inaccurate or incomplete information, telephone calls that were not returned or were returned too late, or the inability to talk directly with the company president. Also, a reporter sometimes believes that he or she was "used" for purposes unrelated to news. For example, a public relations person convinced a newspaper to drop from its obituaries the phrase "in lieu of flowers" when contributions were to be made to a charity instead. Thereafter the paper simply reported in obituaries that contributions could be made to certain charities and omitted any reference to flowers. The policy made some sense — no needless negative image for florists — but the paper had second thoughts when the public relations person received a PR award for bringing about the change.

Relatively few news reporters think of public relations in terms of the Public Relations Society of America, which sponsors numerous workshops and an accreditation program to upgrade industry standards, and few think of public relations personnel as ombudsmen arguing for more disclosure or for social action programs from their employers. Reporters are likely to remember, however, the corporate president who tried to hide poor earnings in the last paragraph of a four-page news release, or the public relations director who denied a merger just hours before it was formally announced.

On the other side, growing hostility toward the news media was apparent in many boardrooms in the 1970s and early 1980s. There are corporation presidents and executives who will not talk to the news media because of what they perceive as sloppy, shallow, inaccurate, or biased reporting.

Unfortunately, many successful business people do not know how to communicate. They compound the problem by hiring amateurs—many of them ex-reporters—who are not competent to draw up long-term public relations goals and objectives and who, as a result, head straight for the word processor to help fill a newsroom wastebasket.

What attitudes does a reporter form about those who send out useless material but decline to comment on significant corporate issues? They are unlikely to be attitudes that lead to a productive news source–news reporter relationship. In evaluating that relationship, probably the one certainty is that public relations people do have a mission: to tell the story of the organizations that issue their paychecks. That mission is not inconsistent with being helpful to reporters. Public relations/public information personnel who are helpful to reporters are often those of most value to their employers because they establish source credibility and status with news reporters. In her Louisiana study, VanSlyke Turk noted that "persuasive public relations tactics do not seem to be as effective with journalists as tactics that involve providing information intended to inform without necessarily persuading."[4]

Also, competent public relations personnel can encourage corporations to include public information concerns in management decision making. A well-prepared news release is no substitute for a corporate communications policy that identifies and addresses concerns of the general audience as well as those of the publics that a corporation deals with, including employees, customers, potential markets, and the news media.

Reporters can do some things to help assure that their relationships with public relations personnel benefit the news audience:

1. Realize that the public relations/public information person has a mission — to tell the story of the employer — but do not assume that the mission necessitates deception. Accurate information about a company's products, number of employees, marketing areas, and public service programs often is useful to readers in stories about the economy, consumer consciousness, and societal trends.

2. Approach the news-gathering situation with a degree of good faith and become acquainted with public relations personnel with whom one might deal on a regular basis. There is a difference between being open-minded and being naive, just as there is a difference between being skeptical and inquisitive instead of being cynical and incredulous. Readers are better served by open-minded but skeptical and inquisitive reporters. As in dealing with other news sources, it is helpful for reporters to talk with public relations sources even when not working on specific stories. Such informal contact may give a reporter a competitive edge when working on a breaking news story, will make the reporter a better judge of a source's credibility, and will lead to a better understanding of the context in which the source operates.

3. Apprise news directors and editors of what appears newsworthy, regardless of its source or potential promotional value. Reporters reading press releases see story elements that those who prepared the releases might have missed. Furthermore, a release that puts someone in a positive light should not be discounted as puffery. An innovation in farm machinery may have far-reaching implications for the nation's economy and social structure.

4. Be cautious and thorough in dealing with press releases and other handouts. Rewriting news releases is a sound practice. In the rewriting process omissions or inaccuracies in a release are more

likely to be noted than if the release is merely edited or run without changes; rewriting makes the story different from accounts used by other news media; rewriting may necessitate contacting other news sources to acquire additional information or to verify information in the release; rewriting often reduces the space or time needed to cover the subject matter. To summarize, rewriting generally better serves the interests of the news audience than does transmitting the release as it arrives in the mail.

ATTENDANCE AT NEWSWORTHY EVENTS

This conventional news source may seem so obvious as to not merit mention. Nevertheless, it needs to be noted that reporters do gather information for the news audience firsthand—instead of being spoon-fed on beats and by public relations personnel—by attending meetings, political rallies, football games, fires, fairs, accidents, and conventions and by reporting societal trends and issues not fully addressed by other conventional sources. Such coverage is essential; it is what much of news reporting will always be about. The reporter gathers news firsthand by observing an event rather than hearing about it from a news source. Beyond that, the strengths of on-the-spot coverage are in its timeliness, human interest, and proximity.

On-the-spot coverage has its shortcomings, however:

1. Coverage by attendance at events is similar to the beat system because many of the events are public meetings or other scheduled happenings that represent points of view similar to those expressed by "officialdom." In deciding what events to cover, the newsroom relies upon many of the criteria used in establishing the beat system.

2. Many news sources have learned to manipulate the news media, contriving what have been termed "pseudo events"—events designed merely to attract media coverage. Furthermore, the increasing importance of the mass media in economic and political terms leads to events being scheduled to accommodate or manipulate media coverage. Baseball's World Series is played at night now

to attract a more lucrative television audience. Collegiate football and basketball games are rescheduled according to television's programming needs. Political conventions are timed so that "exciting" events occur at prime time in the evening or in time to meet the deadlines of leading newspapers. Similarly, news sources may release information or schedule events depending on the importance of the event to the source. Prime time beckons if the event puts the source in a good light; Sunday morning's newspaper or talk show provides a burial ground for unfavorable news.

There is little the news audience or news reporters can do to reverse such trends. Indeed, it can be argued that the marketplace approach to scheduling events often benefits the audience by assuring that the messages reach the largest possible audience. In any case, news reporters and the news audience still should be sensitive to the contrived nature of many on-the-spot events.

3. Coverage by attendance finds the news reporter primarily reacting, chasing to get to where the action is in order to report it. Such reporting results from the conflict orientation in news — defining what is news in terms of the heat it generates instead of the light it sheds on issues and events. And while in theory it should not be a question of one form of coverage or the other, the news audience may be better served by an in-depth look at the causes, results, and treatment of drunken driving than by on-the-scene reports of drunken driving accidents, deaths, and arrests.

At its best, on-the-scene reporting can provide a timely account of an event that should be of significance or interest to the news audience, and it can highlight a stitch or two in the social fabric by calling attention to events and problems that merit further consideration and discussion.

PUBLIC RECORDS AND FREEDOM OF INFORMATION LAWS

Freedom of information (FOI) laws and public record laws are conventional news sources not so much because of their widespread use by news reporters as because access to public records is inherent in our system of government, which requires an informed citizenry. If the citizenry is to be informed and if the government is to be held accountable for decisions made in service to the public, then there must be access to information about decisions made by government agencies.

Two relatively safe observations can be made about news reporters, freedom of information laws, and public records: (1) reporters do not use FOI laws and public records enough, and (2) reporters rely on FOI laws and public records too much. That contradiction results because news reporters do not have the time, inclination, energy, or resources to take advantage of the millions of documents that federal, state, and local laws make available to the public. However, fascination with access provided by FOI laws can cause reporters to neglect other sources of information and perhaps forget that the First Amendment allows them to publish information that FOI laws deny access to.

At the federal level the Freedom of Information Act (FOIA) was passed by Congress and signed by President Johnson in 1968. Amid Watergate-inspired concern with the need to monitor government activity, the act was amended in 1974 and passed over the veto of President Ford, going into effect February 19, 1975. Amendments to the law have been commonplace since then, as Congress seeks to balance access to information about government activities against a host of exemptions to the act. The exemptions seek to safeguard national security, assure some confidentiality for private corporations doing business with the government, and protect the privacy of citizens who are the subjects of government records.

Usually, however, proponents of laws to assure public access to government records and meetings do not want to know national security secrets. Rather, they want to know why one contract for paving county roads was accepted over another, why a new teacher will be added in physical education instead of in music, why a certain person was appointed to complete the unexpired term of a city council member who resigned. Although those may seem mundane matters, such decisions affect the lives of millions of citizens each day.

Lack of use by the press?   The value of the Freedom of Information Act was recognized by private interest groups well before the measure was widely used by the news media. Consumer advocate Ralph Nader used FOI measures to unearth evidence of irresponsibility by major manufacturers of consumer goods. Julius Duscha, in his article "Nader's Raiders Put the Washington Press Corps to Shame," noted how:

> the press is almost totally oriented to reacting to events, or, in too many cases, to pseudo events carefully contrived for press coverage. . . . The hundreds of reporters who make up the Washington press corps still spend an inordinate amount of time serving up rewrites of White House and agency handouts. . . . Nader and his forces are doing no more than what good reporters are supposed to do. His operations are what good newspapering ought to be all about. . . . First must come the extensive study of the background of an issue. . . . Then follows the interviewing of key sources. . . . Finally there are the conclusions to be drawn and the courses of action to be charted. Why is the press generally unwilling to do the kind of in-depth investigative work that is the guts of the approach to public issues? . . . The major reason is the way editors and reporters are oriented toward the reporting of events.[5]

Press performance may not have improved much since Duscha's indictment in the 1970s. Harold C. Relyea, who monitored FOI concerns and worked with the Congressional Research Service in the Library of Congress, reported in the late 1980s that the press accounted for only 5 to 8 percent of FOIA requests for information, while the business community accounted for 50 to 60 percent.[6] The value of the FOIA is documented, however, by such publications as *Former Secrets: Government Records Made Public Through the Freedom of Information Act*[7] and by the fact that Relyea's report of low formal usage by the press may be misleading. The mere existence of the FOIA provides ammunition for reporters and citizens who ask to see government records. These records usually are provided without a formal request being made.

New York Times columnist William Safire declared that the FOIA "has done more to inhibit the abuse of government power and to protect the citizen from unlawful snooping and arrogant harassment than any legislation in our lifetime."[8]

While the sheer volume of government records at the federal, state, and local levels may be an impediment to their use, news reporters and the general public are seldom interested in seeing all of a government agency's records. A tailored request for specific records on a particular topic can save the time of the reporter and of public officials. That request can be as simple as asking to see the minutes of the last school board meeting, the record of mileage expenses paid to sheriff's deputies or of salaries paid to school teachers, or records of how many substitute teachers are used by school districts. Such records are routinely kept by public agencies, and various state laws require that they be made available. Almost any question one can ask about government — the public's business — has an answer lurking in public records. To begin to find it, all the reporter has to do is ask.

Over-reliance by the Press? Laws on access to public records are not ends in themselves, yet their symbolic value often is emphasized by advocates of "the public's right to know" in defense of news reporters' efforts to get information. Such rhetoric borders on overkill, given the vast amount of information available but not routinely used by the news media or the public. Associate Justice Hans Linde of the Oregon Supreme Court cautioned against right-to-know oratory:

> The press should not submerge the tough right to publish in a wishy-washy slogan of the people's right to know. I know it lets the press sound noble. But to measure the rights of the media by the rights of the audience is a trap. . . . The reverse implication is that the media's constitutional right to publish something is no greater than the public's constitutional right to have it disclosed. There are many things that the public has no such right to have disclosed but that the First Amendment will nevertheless protect one in publishing.[9]

In addition to Linde's constitutional approach, there should be concern with over-reliance on public records simply because the records have an aura of being tangible and more credible than other sources. Certainly in legal cases use of a public record is a better defense than comments from an anonymous source. But one problem with printed records is that errors take on lives of their own and once in print or in a data bank are difficult to update or correct.

One popular illustration of the canonization of error deals with the history of the bathtub as American humorist and reporter H. L. Mencken developed it in a satirical piece written for the *New York Evening Mail* in 1917. Elements of Mencken's fictional history still keep popping up in columns and other references. Readers are led to believe, for example, that there was a dispute in the nineteenth century about the health hazards of bathing following the bathtub's introduction in England in 1828 or that Millard Fillmore was the first American president to have a bathtub in the White House. These and other bits of history sprang from the imagination of Mencken. Who in fact was the first president to have a bathtub in the White House? It may not matter now: Fillmore has won the day. But if "James Polk" were printed here, as an answer, would that be more convincing than if someone simply told you it was Polk?

Quotations from scripture will vary, of course, from one version of the Bible to another, as in some cases the order of the Ten Commandments varies. Likewise, Hamlet did not say, "Alas! poor Yorick. I knew him well"; rather, he says, "Alas! poor Yorick! I knew him, Horatio."

Thus it is useful to verify information in a public record, just as it is important to verify information from a human news source. Having the record in hand, the news reporter might want to review its information with the person responsible for generating the information. That may be particularly helpful in dealing with budgets, medical reports, highway plans, and census data.

The courts are one governmental jurisdiction, however, in which the printed and public record cannot be discussed routinely with the person producing it. Judicial opinions, particularly at the appellate level, are expected to speak for themselves. Judges will not explain an opinion to a news reporter because opinions and dissents could become unwieldy if each jurist gave an interpretation of the opinion in addition to what was in writing. The opinions of course can be discussed with the attorneys involved and with a court's public information person. For the news audience, problems in the interpretation of court decisions are compounded when news stories on court rulings are written without the reporter having read the full text of the decision, perhaps because of deadline pressures. Consequently some nuances or interpretations of law are missed in the news coverage.

In reporting on the courts, as in other areas of news coverage, the audience is best served by news reporters who rely on a number of news-gathering methods—covering the court as a beat, providing timely news coverage of decisions, remaining in contact with public relations and public information personnel, and making use of public records. News stories, like tapestries, can be woven with a variety of strong threads, making the finished product of more substance and of more worth than if a single approach were used.

Nonconventional news sources

Nonconventional news sources are not necessarily strange, exotic, or newly discovered ways of gathering information (although some could fit into any or all of those categories). Such sources simply may not be fully utilized, understood, or relied upon, particularly when conventional sources can generate far more information than the news media can accommodate. A news organization may not have the expertise, facilities, or staff time to make use of the insights available through precision journalism and the use of databases. Few papers can afford to invest seventeen months of a reporter's time in living in a ghetto apartment in order to gain the confidence of poor teenaged mothers and report their stories. The *Washington Post* did, and reporter Leon Dash, a finalist for a Pulitzer Prize in 1987, said:

> There was no quicker way to do it. The problem is that we went along for months until I had established a relationship, and then everyone changed, dramatically changed the first story they had told me. They directly contradicted their public face.[10]

The poorer members of society may be at one end of the news source spectrum in that they wish to avoid news media attention. At the other end are bizarre news sources, such as terrorist organizations who hold the media as figurative hostages. The nonconventional sources discussed below will range from computer-driven databases to life-threatening and life-taking terrorists.

PRECISION JOURNALISM

The term "precision journalism" represents the introduction of social and behavioral science research techniques into news reporting. The case for this improvement in reporting methods was made more than a dozen years ago in *Precision Journalism*: *A Reporter's Introduction to Social Science Methods* by Philip Meyer and in *Handbook of Reporting Methods* by Maxwell McCombs, Donald Shaw, and David Grey, but the concept remains nonconventional in most newsrooms. In his opening chapter, "The Need for New Tools," Meyer wrote:

> It used to be said that journalism is history in a hurry. . . . To cope with the acceleration of social change in today's world, journalism must become social science in a hurry. . . . The ground rules are no different from those on which we've always operated: find the facts, tell what they mean and do it without wasting time. If there are new tools to enable us to perform this task with greater power, accuracy and insight, then we should make the most of them.[11]

McCombs et al. wrote of translating reporting goals and tasks into the framework of research in sociology and psychology:

> Our central premise is that this translation will enhance the quality of news reporting in two ways. First, behavioral

> science methodology makes possible a whole realm of description that is simply not feasible using the traditional interview or paper-and-pencil techniques of interviewing. . . . Second, news reporting is also enhanced by behavioral science methods that lead the reporter beyond description to explanation.[12]

The methodology these authors write of includes survey research, random samples, sensitive interviewing techniques, and field experiments. Reporters are well advised to acquaint themselves with such methods because their use can improve the accuracy and reliability of sampling public opinion and because even if news reporters are not using these methods, others, including news sources, are.

With the computer now commonplace in most newsrooms and with the availability of relatively inexpensive computer time, using survey research has become about as convenient as sending two or three reporters out to interview passersby on the street. Moreover, survey research promises greater accuracy. A field experiment can be something as simple as testing the efficiency of zip codes through systematic mailing of letters without codes and with five- and nine-digit codes. With relative ease newsrooms can draw a statistically sound sample of the community to survey their opinions and provide a check against the accuracy of responses when the newspaper invites all readers to "tell us what you think."

Even if news agencies do not routinely use these methods, reporters need to be better acquainted with them for the sake of the news audience. Almost any political candidate or interest group can cook up a poll or study to "document" widespread public support. Reporters need to know enough about research techniques to evaluate the newsworthiness of such findings and to tell readers and viewers why certain data may be questionable. For instance, the accuracy problems of phone-in "public opinion" polls are obvious. Many news media have taken what are for them giant steps forward in reporting a margin of error along with poll results. The existence of a margin of error at least suggests some care was taken with the poll. (A margin of error is reported in terms of plus and minus percentages. For example, a poll might have a margin of error of plus or minus 5 percent. That means if the poll shows a breakdown of opinion to be 53 to 47 percent, the swing could be as much as 58 to 42 or 48 to 52, a 5-percent change in the results for each side.)

Precision journalism is not a panacea; it adds some problems of its own. Reporters enamored of survey research, for example, may immerse the news audience in irrelevant information. Political campaign coverage tells us who would win if Ms. X were running against Mr. Y today. But neither of them is running, and the election is not today but two years hence. The report of the contrived election comes at the expense of the reporter's time and of news space that might be better allocated on behalf of the news audience. When incorrectly used, high-powered tools may only bring high-powered reporting mistakes that are more devious and difficult to discern because the potentially erroneous report carries the label "scientific" or is sanctified as computer output. A considerable burden remains on the reporter to use reporting methods wisely when he or she moves "beyond description to explanation."

Databases. Information about human activities and the human condition often can be retrieved through databases — high-speed and relatively comprehensive reference and record systems. In its simplest form a database provides through a computer quick and easy access to reference systems, such as the *Readers' Guide to Periodical Literature*. Instead of leafing through bound volumes of such a reference work, the reporter simply enters the database via computer and gets the desired information in a matter of seconds or minutes instead of hours.

The 1988 catalog of Dialog information services, a common database distributor, listed a selection of 300 databases with more than 150 million records and search costs estimated at about five to seventeen dollars for ten minutes. Material available ranged from directory listings of people and corporations to complete texts of articles and reports.

A database on child abuse provided access to about 17,000

records compiled by the National Center of Child Abuse and Neglect in the U.S. Department of Health and Human Services. The records covered such areas as research projects, legal references, bibliographies, and service programs. One of the business-oriented databases, Moody's Corporate News-U.S., offered some 236,000 records "of business and financial information on approximately 13,000 public-held U.S. corporations," including banks, insurance companies, and public utilities.

Because databases are relatively new ways of organizing information, the records are usually current, but historical data might not have been computerized yet. The user must rely on the judgment of the publishers in determining what information merits database treatment. Furthermore, the database provides the information the user asks for, not necessarily the information the user wants or needs. The user needs to understand database protocol and to phrase requests to extract the desired information. At about eighty dollars an hour there is not much margin for just wandering around sampling this and that. Nor, of course, are such records error-free.

The availability of computer-stored information makes it possible for reporters to find or verify information that could not be dealt with before. For example, to document a government scandal in Rhode Island reporters had to analyze thousands of loans, a task that simply was not feasible without the use of a computer, as indicated by these two paragraphs from the *Providence Sunday Journal* of June 2, 1985:

> Children of some of the state's most powerful political and financial figures received low-rate mortgages from a secret fund maintained by the Rhode Island Housing and Mortgage Finance Corporation. . . .
> Although 8½-percent loans issued in a 1979 program had supposedly been used up within a year, a *Journal-Bulletin* computer analysis of 25,000 RIHMFC mortgages found some homeowners getting those loans as late as last November.

MINORITIES AND THE DISENFRANCHISED AS NEWS SOURCES

Conventional news sources are weighted toward the "establishment" or, in less pejorative terms, the majority point of view or the status quo. Recognizing this, the Commission on Freedom of the Press in its now classic report said that one of the requirements of the mass media was to project "a representative picture of the constituent groups in the society." The commission's concern was that some groups were stereotyped in the media:

> If Chinese appear in a succession of pictures as sinister drug addicts and militarists, an image of China is built which needs to be balanced by another. If the Negro appears in the stories published in magazines of national circulation only as a servant, if the children figure constantly in radio dramas as impertinent and ungovernable brats—the image of the Negro and the American child is distorted.[13]

Concern should be not only with stereotypes in reporting but also with assuring access to the media so that minority groups might find more opportunities to participate in making the decisions that affect their lives. Tom Wicker of the *New York Times* noted that reliance on official or conventional news sources could be counterproductive:

> We have to overcome or at least reduce and balance our reliance on official sources of news, which I regard as the gravest professional and intellectual weakness of American journalism. . . . A lot of what's happening in the country today, a lot of what is most vital in people's lives, isn't institutionalized so there's no official spokesman for it. If you stick to covering the official sources, inevitably you miss a lot of important things that are going on elsewhere. So, for instance, the press largely missed one of the great migrations of human history, the migration of black people out of the South and into the cities. . . . And until Ralph Nader made something sensational out of it, we missed the rise in consumer consciousness; now, ironically, we've made something of an official source out of Ralph Nader. It's the way we like to work.[14]

Barriers to substantive news coverage. "The way we like to work" does little to facilitate substantive news coverage of the disenfranchised in society. Reporters are "far better at simply discovering the poor than we are at explaining the cause of poverty and exploring the solutions." Michael Moss, a reporter for the *Atlanta Journal and Constitution*, offered that observation in a review of how journalists cover poverty as a news story.[15] Too much coverage, he said, was in the nature of "spot" news coverage: it is cold in the city, so do a story on the homeless; it is Thanksgiving, so do a story showing that the city has a heart and is helping the malnourished; a grand jury has issued an indictment, so do a story on welfare fraud. Such stories meet the criteria of news since they are timely and have human interest and can be treated in hit-and-run fashion.

Opportunities for continuing and in-depth coverage of issues suffer because responsibility for covering the disenfranchised as a beat is not vested in a single news reporter or editor; because periodic, seasonal, or feature coverage is considered adequate; because coverage of the disenfranchised takes on overtones of advocacy, which makes reporters and editors leery since they are vulnerable to being used; because for most of its history American journalism has been in the hands of white, middle-class males whose upbringing and experience did little to encourage recognizing, understanding, and interpreting issues of race and class.

There is a scarcity of reliable and articulate news sources, be they people or printed materials. The disenfranchised themselves almost by definition do not or cannot use the "established" language or the "established" channels to facilitate news coverage. As for printed records, Moss cautioned:

> Few are the reporters who know that the government uses two different sets of numbers and systems to determine who is statistically poor and who qualifies for the government aid programs. Fewer still are those who can sort through such terms as illegitimacy, birth rate, birth ratio, and fertility, which when used incorrectly—as they sometimes are by experts who have ideologies to support—give a skewed picture

of such critical issues as teenage motherhood and the trends in pregnancy.[16]

Moss concludes that for these and other reasons

we return to the regular news about affairs of state and people of fame and fortune, slamming the journalistic door on the 57 million Americans living near or below the poverty line until someone in the newsroom decides . . . to "get some poverty stuff."[17]

News coverage not a cure, but . . . The shortcomings of news coverage constitute a symptom, not the cause, of social problems in poverty, discrimination, illiteracy, care of the mentally ill, health care crises, drug addiction, penal institutions, and child abuse — to list just a few. If such problems are to be addressed in meaningful, long-term fashion, then news coverage must contribute to the process by keeping the news audience abreast of the issues. Moss asserts that "the poor and their world offer a new frontier for reporting that is every bit as challenging and demanding of bravery and boldness as covering war or politics or the next scandal."[18]

The need, challenges, and rewards of such news coverage are illustrated by the work of Jonathan Kozol in such books as *Death at an Early Age, Illiterate America*, and *Homeless Families in America*. Insights to social problems need not be monopolized by book-length treatment. The news media, after all, reach a far wider audience. The news coverage may require an increased investment of newsroom time and resources. However, the coverage also can be built into newsroom routines by developing nonconventional news sources and by reporting the impacts of building code changes, zoning laws, health care policies, and other governmental decisions on all segments of society.

The composition of the newsroom is important, too. News coverage of women has gone beyond the kitchen-and-apron stage partly because there are now more women in newsrooms, and that trend is likely to continue because more than 60 percent of the undergraduates in journalism and mass communications programs are female. Efforts to bring more racial minorities into the newsrooms also have gained support from news media associations. What happens in such transformations is that not only are there new reporters in the newsroom but the incoming reporters develop new sources, thus providing a broader, more representative pool of information for the news audience.

A starting point for change may be better-informed coverage of societal problems, but the insights of minorities and the disenfranchised are also essential in the day-to-day news coverage of decisions by groups such as city councils and school boards. That is why editors and news directors usually learn not to limit women and minority reporters to covering "women's" or "minority group" issues. Such reporters and their news sources constitute too rich a resource to be pigeonholed.

TERRORISTS AS NEWS SOURCES

News coverage of terrorism offers a worst-case scenario for the news reporter–news source relationship. That relationship is turned on its head as the news source demands coverage at gunpoint. What we have discussed about other elements of the reporter-source relationship, such as the reporter serving as an intermediary between news sources (the government and the terrorist) or the reporter protecting and promoting news sources becomes distorted and macabre when placed in the context of an act of terrorism. In much of news reporting the concern is that the reporter not become a participant in the event or issue being covered. The reporter's three roles are those of observer, intermediary, and participant, and the journalist does all he or she can to minimize the role of participant and to structure the role of intermediary to serve the interests of the news audience. In coverage of terrorism, however, the order and emphasis of those roles is almost reversed. Terrorist demands often define the news media as participants in the event, and the news-reporting role may become secondary or even tertiary.

A definition of terrorism developed by Professor L. John

Martin of the University of Maryland will help to begin this discussion of terrorists as news sources:

> For an act to be terrorism, we must answer "yes" to the following three questions:
>
> 1. Is the violence or threat of political violence an *intentionally public* act?
> 2. Is it a means to a known or implied end beyond the act itself [such as demanding the release of people from prison or seeking a public forum for the airing of views]?
> 3. Are there announced or implied beneficiaries other than the perpetrators of the act? (. . . It cannot just be a kidnap for ransom, for example, with the money going to the kidnapers for their personal use.)[19]

For purposes of our discussion it is assumed that the act of terrorism is fairly prolonged, lasting long enough to involve the presence of news media covering the event. Also, although it seems too obvious to warrant stating, it is assumed that the act is a crime. The second assumption is important because the commission of a crime changes some of the rules of news coverage and increases the authority of the government agency involved. (Police at a crime scene have more authority over a reporter than does a school superintendent at a school board meeting.)

Terrorism is not a twentieth-century phenomenon, but it has been cast in a new light because of news media coverage.

Three acts of terrorism

1. In September 1976 Croatian nationalists seeking independence from Yugoslavia hijacked a jetliner flying from New York to Chicago and demanded that the exact text of their manifesto be published on the front page in the next day's *New York Times, Los Angeles Times, Washington Post, Chicago Tribune*, and *International Herald Tribune*. If the manifesto were not published, the terrorists said, a bomb would be detonated in a "highly busy location." A policeman had already been killed while trying to disarm a terrorist bomb in a New York subway station.

The American newspapers complied with the request; the next

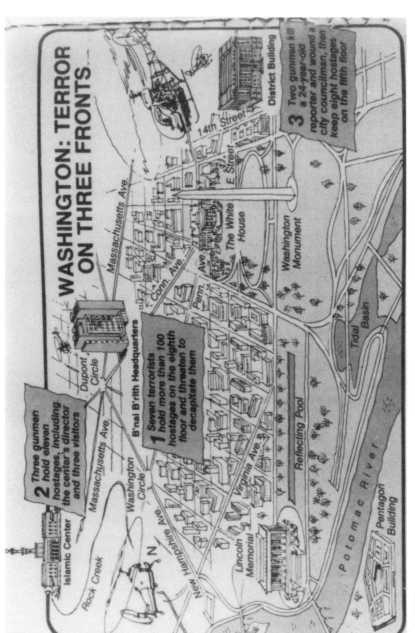

WASHINGTON: TERROR ON THREE FRONTS

1 Seven terrorists hold more than 100 hostages on the eighth floor and threaten to decapitate them

2 Three gunmen hold eleven hostages, including the center's director and three visitors

3 Two gunmen kill a 24-year-old reporter and wound a city councilman, then keep eight hostages on the fifth floor

District Building

14th Street

E Street

The White House

Washington Monument

Tidal Basin

Reflecting Pool

Potomac River

Pentagon Building

Lincoln Memorial

Virginia Ave.

Penn. Ave.

Conn. Ave.

Massachusetts Ave.

Dupont Circle

B'nai B'rith Headquarters

Washington Circle

Massachusetts Ave.

New Hampshire Ave.

Islamic Center

Rock Creek

N

Credit: Ib Ohlsson.

day's *International Herald Tribune*, published in Paris, was already on the streets at the time the demand was made. The papers that complied with the request did so partly because the manifesto itself had some newsworthy elements and because, more importantly, the terrorists had already taken one life—that of the policeman—so the threat had credibility. "I wasn't going to have any other deaths on my conscience," said William F. Thomas, editor of the *Los Angeles Times*.[20]

The Croatian hijacking was one of the first acts directly to involve the news media. The newspapers responded individually and under time pressure since press runs for the next day's papers were already under way. (That meant the papers did not have to run the manifesto in every edition.) The terrorist act was not imitated, perhaps because other terrorists recognized that television coverage better met their needs. Editors shied away from making any statements about what they would do in future cases, except to suggest that a news medium could not allow itself to be taken hostage and to oppose any proposed uniform code of conduct that might violate First Amendment rights.

2. The news media came under criticism for coverage of a March 1977 terrorist act in which 135 hostages were held for thirty-nine hours in three Washington, D.C., buildings—the Islamic Center, the B'nai B'rith headquarters, and the District Building (or city hall). The leader of a Hanafi Muslim sect, Hamaas Abdul Khaalis, was seeking revenge for the 1973 murder of his five children by black muslims. The only fatally injured victim this time was not one of the hostages but a news reporter, Maurice Williams, 24, of radio station WLUR. Williams was struck down by a shotgun blast when he and city officials entered the District Building at the start of the episode. Besides his death, the Hanafi case is significant because it was one of the first and one of the few incidents in which news coverage threatened rescue efforts and might have interfered with police.[21]

A television report showed a basket being lifted by a rope to rescue people whose presence in one building had eluded the terrorists. The people finally did escape, but terrorists in the building apparently were told of the presence of other potential hostages by accomplices who were monitoring news coverage.

In a live radio interview a news reporter asked the terrorist leader, "Have you set a deadline?" The absence of any deadline had been taken as an encouraging sign by police.

Another newsman interviewing Khaalis by phone suggested that maybe the police were trying to "trick" him or were "pulling a fast one" by pretending to negotiate in good faith while readying a strike force. That suggestion so enraged Khaalis that he threatened to begin executing hostages.

One of the hostages, Charles Fenyvesi, was editor of the *National Jewish Monthly*, published by B'nai B'rith. He wrote of the ordeal:

> We did have periodic visits from Khaalis, who prefaced each appearance with this announcement: "Everybody in the world is trying to talk to me." He was elated as he informed us — and our guards — that newsmen called him from as far as England, France, Africa, Australia, and, of course, from all over the United States. . . .
>
> The media were our other enemy, I have learned from conversations with fellow hostages. Some say that the media were the enemy because they sensationalized our ordeal. . . . Other ex-hostages . . . argue that the media were the enemy because they left the impression that the gunmen had been kind and merciful. And, finally, there is a consensus that the media provided a forum for the anti-Semitic rage of the Hanafis and that some of the reporting, particularly some interpretive pieces, reflected more compassion for the terrorists than for their victims.[22]

3. On June 14, 1985, Shiite Moslems hijacked TWA flight 847 on the way from Athens to Rome. Two members of Islamic Jihad (Holy War) forced the pilot to fly between Algiers and Beirut four times. They tortured and killed a U.S. Navy diver and released 113 passengers but held 39 Americans hostage until June 30. In Beirut members of Amal, the main Shiite faction in Lebanon, took over

from the hijackers. The terrorists were seeking the release of 776 fellow Shiites held prisoner in Israel.[23]

News media coverage during these two weeks was criticized as "terrorvision" and "media terrorism":

> TV people did much that they could be proud of: we saw individual examples of hard-working, intelligent anchors; dedicated, physically courageous field reporters; incisive commentators, concerned producers and feats of technical wizardry. But when the parts are all added up, the TV system collectively went wrong. It was as if the organizational zeal and Mideast politics transformed television into extremist terrorvision, in the fashion of Dr. Jekyll and Mr. Hyde.[24]

Critics focused on many problems with the coverage. News media emphasis on the Shiites held prisoner by Israel made negotiations difficult. The coverage ignored other demands and created a situation in which neither the United States nor Israel would have room to compromise or even, in Israel's case, to proceed with some releases that reportedly were planned before the hijacking. The atmosphere was one of competitive frenzy with the stakes in TV ratings high:

> Competition is fierce, the pressures for scoops intense, and the scramble for advantage sometimes riotous. So riotous that during one press conference the armed terrorists had to retreat in disorder with their hostages before a mob of jostling, screaming newsmen.[25]

In an interview with Amal leader Nabih Berri, David Hartman, then host of ABC's *Good Morning America*, asked if Berri had "any final words" for President Reagan. That sounded to some like TV was conducting its own negotiations. Incredibly, some sought to explain away Hartman's involvement by arguing that he was on the salary of the network's entertainment division, not the news division![26] CBS anchorman Dan Rather was said to be guilty of living-room diplomacy when he advised viewers that "Berri told me that if Israel agrees to release its Shiite prisoners, a third country could arrange an exchange."

In a review of news coverage of terrorism, Michael J. O'Neill, a past president of the American Society of Newspaper Editors, noted the contradictions in coverage of the TWA hijacking and offered a glimpse, too, at the role of reporters as intermediaries:

> Television initially heightened public fears with its suspenseful, dramatized coverage, but later dissipated those fears with pictures showing that the hostages were in no immediate danger, allowing the government more time to grope toward a solution. Television broke a dozen journalistic laws when it became a participant in the crisis and supplied its own celebrity negotiators, yet it also was a help. It set up the communications, then connected all the parties to each other in such a disguised way that no one had to talk publicly to anyone else. It relayed positions back and forth until everyone understood the settlement terms.[27]

News-reporting concerns. As difficult as news coverage of terrorist activities is, and as distressing and as irresponsible as the coverage may be at times, there are worse alternatives to the risks of news coverage and dealing with terrorists as news sources: such as no coverage at all, or coverage under strict governmental control. Blackouts or government dictation of coverage, even if practicable, are so contrary to the ideal of having an informed citizenry that imposition of such restrictions conveys a sense of surrender to terrorism.

The fear that news media coverage might encourage copycat terrorist acts is an understandable one, but thus far has not been substantiated or even well supported. One might counter that fear with the hypothesis that media coverage of terrorist events serves as a safety valve, reducing the violence committed by such dissidents. The continuing violence in Northern Ireland is a distressing illustration of how terrorism continues even with strict controls and government censorship of news coverage. Discussion may be better served by moving from hypothetical concerns to the problems of coverage when terrorist acts occur.

Despite the problems with news coverage, none of the hostages died as a result of irresponsible news reporting in the above illustrations. That may be a matter of dumb luck, or it may be evidence that news reporters recognize what is at stake in news coverage of terrorism — as in Beirut when the media did not identify government officials among the hostages.

The risks of news media involvement as quasi negotiators should be better recognized by now. The TWA hijacking was an ordeal for the news media as well, one with lessons that should sober reporters as to the limits and uses of news reporting.

Recognition of a terrorist act as a crime may provide some focus for news decision making. News coverage should not aid criminal activity. Government agencies have powers to restrict news coverage of crime scenes; exercise of those powers is restrained because news coverage may serve as a safety valve and may even become a bargaining chip for the release of hostages. That places the news media in a peculiar relationship with both the conventional and the nonconventional news sources, but as has already been noted the nature of terrorist activities does make some standard reporter-source relationships distorted and macabre.

Beginning in the late 1970's the broadcast networks sought to address the difficulties of such news coverage with general guidelines, as these excerpts suggest:

CBS: "There can be no specific self-executing rules for the handling of terrorist/hostage stories [beyond] the normal tests of news judgment. Nevertheless, there must be thoughtful, conscientious care and restraint."

NBC: "We must balance, delicately, an obligation to keep the public informed, an obligation to avoid being used and an obligation not to exacerbate or sensationalize the situation."

ABC: "We must do nothing that could jeopardize the lives of

hostages, or interfere with efforts by authorities to secure their safe release. We must guard against efforts by terrorists to use, or manipulate us for their own ends."

Similar guidelines have been drafted by newspapers, partly in response to questions about news coverage. That there has been irresponsible coverage no one can deny. But coverage of a boring city council meeting can be irresponsible, too; the immediate effects are less easy to discern, perhaps, but in a system of government based on an informed electorate continual irresponsibility of media coverage on any important subject is pernicious. The answer is not to have less coverage or none at all. The answer, rather, is to have better news coverage.

Improved coverage of terrorism might result from attention to these concerns:

1. As a matter of restraint news coverage needs to focus on the news event — in most cases the seizure of hostages — and not on exclusive stories or pseudo events to hype the coverage. In routine news coverage the enterprising reporter's quest is for an angle or element of the story that the competition does not have or for the question that the competition does not ask. In the case of terrorism such coverage shifts the focus from the primary news event, and the quest for scoops may lead to news coverage defined by the epithet *terrorvision.*

2. The consequences of news coverage, as noted in chapter 1, are the least helpful guide for journalists. Usually the effects of supposedly harmful information or an error in reporting can be offset by corrections or additional information to put the record straight. In the case of terrorism, however, if a mistake is made, additional information may not carry such healing or palliative powers. The risks involved are immediate and direct.

3. The news reporter should not be deluded by self-definition as an impartial observer and recorder. Journalists may be viewed by government as a potentially helpful but troubling nuisance or by terrorists as an agent of the establishment to be manipulated. The

sources are not playing the "neutral" game, and what information is reported to the news audience may be shaped by their demands. The terrorist may dictate the nature of coverage by fear; the government, by exercise of police powers at a crime scene. Such controls over the press are unavoidable and also unfortunate. They are unavoidable because of the risks of loss of life; they are unfortunate because news coverage can help resolve crises, as O'Neill noted in the role of the press as intermediary in the TWA hijacking.

4. News coverage of terrorism generally is coverage of the symptoms of global ills. O'Neill calls for the practice of what he terms "preventive journalism," which in essence is improved news coverage of foreign affairs to alert society to the root causes of conflict instead of focusing on the conflict itself. He writes that "reporters must be more than the sentinels of reaction, waiting to cover violence and disaster while another unseen world throbs with warnings we do not hear. They need to lead us into that world and help us detect the sounds of future crises."[28]

5. Finally, in considering news coverage of a terrorist act, the question is asked: "Is the reporter an American first or a journalist first?" That question is shorthand for the many questions confronting the reporter. It may be deceptive, however, in that the two roles of citizen and journalist are not necessarily contradictory nor easily separable. The reporter may serve the nation best by being reluctant to abandon principles—including responsibility to the news audience for an accurate and sensitive report—that provide an anchor in times of turmoil. Much of what sets the United States apart from other nations rests on the First Amendment.[29] Abandoning such rights in times of stress can shape a terrorist victory.

Summary

A survey of conventional news sources includes such traditional news-gathering methods as the use of standard beats and assignments, reliance on public relations and promotional personnel, attendance at newsworthy events, and use of freedom of information laws and public records. While much of such coverage may be viewed as routine and as reinforcing the status quo, such coverage is unavoidable, necessary, and even desirable in helping develop an informed citizenry and in monitoring the governmental and private agencies whose decisions affect our lives. Such news coverage, however, remains only a part — granted a large part — of the demands for accurate, responsible, and comprehensive news coverage. To make the societal picture complete, news reporters need to be sensitive to opportunities provided by the relatively unconventional methods of precision journalism and need to improve news coverage of minority groups and the disenfranchised. Calls for "better news coverage" require that reporters recognize and respond to the challenges in covering a wide variety of social issues and problems. Part of the answer to providing such coverage is to develop "unconventional" newsrooms that reflect more than the white, male, middle-class view of society.

Issues involved in news coverage of terrorist activities are not fully understood, and the questions are not easily answered. Fortunately the news media seem to have stumbled through a decade of such coverage without causing significant harm and at times have provided helpful insight and perspective. Having no coverage or only government-dictated coverage of terrorist activities is a worse alternative than placing upon reporters the burden of informed and responsible coverage. But the still better option is for the news media and the news audience to be sensitive to needs for information about societal and global ills and not only for information about the conflicts and violence resulting from those problems.

Reporters and sources, or ghouls and victims?

Testing the limits in reporter-source relationships

Introduction

A dictionary — Webster's again — defines a ghoul as "a legendary evil being that robs graves and feeds on corpses" and adds that the term also can be applied to "one suggestive of a ghoul." Aggrieved news sources and press critics probably are not aware of such literal definitions when they call reporters "ghouls" or "vultures," but they know what they mean. They mean they are outraged by the insensitivity of reporters who appear to covet and compete for news coverage of tragedy.

In the play *Inherit the Wind* attorney Clarence Darrow tells a cynical reporter, "You never pushed a noun against a verb except to blow up something." Charles Fenyvesi, a hostage in the Hanafi Muslim terrorist episode, wrote, "The press has no concern for human life, I hear the charge again and again. The press is after blood, gore and mayhem. The press revels in sickness and perversity."[1]

Similar remarks come from inside the press. Eric Schmitt of the Washington bureau of the *New York Times* commented on coverage of the wake of David Kennedy, a son of the late Robert F. Kennedy. Schmitt told how reporters, photographers, and television crews hounded the mourners:

143

It shocked my sense of civility that the press or the public believed it had a rightful place to be there. Instead of what should have been a private moment for the family, the press declared the sad gathering of Kennedys a newsworthy event. . . . I felt ashamed to be a journalist. I felt like an accomplice to a ghoulish rite of passage.[2]

These criticisms introduce a new dimension to the discussion of news reporter–news source relationships. In many of the preceding chapters, news sources often were voluntary sources or persons expected to provide information to the general public because of their positions, areas of expertise, or insights. Many of the news sources were not news subjects themselves, rather they were asked to comment on another person or to share insights when the real spotlight was on an issue or event. Now the news sources are news subjects themselves, and some are thrust into the public spotlight by tragedy or as victims of crime, disease, or other misfortunes. Other sources, such as political candidates or celebrities, have a place in the public spotlight by choice but still resent news coverage of issues considered to be private or irrelevant to public roles.

GROUND RULES FOR DISCUSSION

This discussion of sensitive or controversial areas of reporter-source relationships has six ground rules:

1. *The latitude of the First Amendment.* Under the First Amendment to the U.S. Constitution and similar provisions in state constitutions Americans have wide latitude of expression. In fact community mores, civic responsibilities, family concerns, and respect for others place greater restrictions on expression than do courts and government agencies. Nevertheless, the First Amendment is the bulwark for free expression, and the test of such freedom is the right to express a hated idea; few object when someone praises the virtues of our society.

2. *Risks and restraints.* The U.S. system of government is a system of risks. There are great risks in allowing citizens the right to vote. There are risks in assuming that a person is innocent until

proven guilty of a crime. There are risks in the Fifth Amendment protection against self-incrimination. There are risks in safeguarding First Amendment rights. In some instances steps have been taken to reduce risks: convicted felons lose the right to vote; high bail may be set to assure that an innocent person appears for trial; obscenity is denied First Amendment protection. However, as restraints are imposed and risks supposedly lessened, the nature of society changes, moving — perhaps ever so slightly, perhaps in giant steps — away from a system that values individual rights to one that increases the power of government agencies over individuals. In general, allowing abuse of rights — abuse that is relatively rare — is preferable to setting restraints.

3. *Access to public records.* Citizens give government certain responsibilities and duties. To monitor the government they have created, citizens have access to government records, such as budgets, minutes of meetings, salaries of public officials, legislation, and arrest records. Such access is symbolic of the system of government, helping ensure that laws and procedures are uniformly followed and enforced and that public funds are appropriately spent. Public access to arrest records, for example, helps ensure that the nation or a community does not have a Gestapo-type police force empowered to make secret arrests. And while one might question whether a newspaper should publish records of arrests for drunken driving when those arrested have not yet been convicted, such openness is more a matter for celebration. When a member of a family is unaccountably late, for example, Americans have a measure of confidence that the person is not being held secretly by police — an assurance that most citizens of the world have not had.

4. *A preference for openness.* In a participatory democracy truth is preferable to falsehood, openness preferable to secrecy, and verified information preferable to rumor. Such preferences may be fraught with risks and potential harm. But the logic of the preferences is that it is better for a news medium to report that a school principal has been charged with child molestation — to take a troubling issue — than for the community to be rife with rumors

about why the principal suddenly was suspended or placed on leave. The rumors may be worse than a news report based on public record, and the principal is, after all, innocent until proven guilty. The latter condition may draw snickers, but belief in the innocence of a person is not a comfortable myth to be ignored when it suits the public; it is one of the frameworks of the judicial system and supports the need for openness and access to information.

5. *A public-press distinction.* Generally it is the responsibility of the news media to report information and the responsibility of the public, if it wishes, to act on that information. Sometimes the public is left out of the equation, as when the news media decide not to provide information on sensitive issues or when the public response is presumed to be a foregone conclusion. Press reporting of presidential candidate Gary Hart's extramarital affairs serves as an illustration. For decades the press had not provided such information on public figures. When it did, Hart responded by dropping out of the race for the Democratic party's nomination, only to recognize later that the public had been left out. Eventually he reentered the race to let the public have its say; perhaps the result was the same, but at least the process had been played out. Simply because the press reports an issue or event does not mean the public has to respond or will respond in an expected fashion.

6. *The nature of the news media.* The news media are pervasive in American society, reporting on all its facets, including the tragic. Partly because of this, many journalists are thin-skinned, sensitive to criticism, and introspective. Consequently, how the news media cover a story sometimes draws more attention than the story itself. When R. Budd Dwyer, the treasurer of Pennsylvania, killed himself at a press conference on January 22, 1987, the news of his death was soon swamped by analysis of what the press could or should have done. Analysis was unavoidable, but it overwhelmed the more poignant and distressing story of the suicide.

The press sometimes exhibits questionable priorities. For example, consider the case of a photographer who

> faced the dilemma of taking pictures or trying to help a woman keep her husband from killing himself. He tried to do both — by taking five shots as he attempted to talk the man out of jumping one hundred feet into the Columbia River and as he yelled at other motorists on the bridge to go for help. But the man soon struggled free from the desperate grip of his wife and jumped to his death.[3]

A dilemma is a choice between two equally unsatisfactory options or two equally compelling alternatives. Perhaps too much is made of the word "dilemma," but — even considering the trauma of the moment — what is so difficult about choosing between trying to save a man's life or taking his picture? Such extreme instances are rare, and they detract from the fact that the American press generally is more restrained and responsible in covering human affairs than is the press of many nations. But persons who are the subject of unwanted press attention may question that judgment or find no solace in it.

Public Figures

The years 1987 and 1988 may not have been watershed years for American politics, but they will prove to be watershed years for the manner in which the news media cover the political process. That is because charges and admissions of adultery, plagiarism, and marijuana use involved presidential candidates, were widely published and discussed, and affected the political campaigns. Voters were told things that previously the press and the politicians had kept to themselves. Previously, such information had not been considered newsworthy because (1) reporters drew a distinction between a public figure's public and private lives, (2) the information was considered irrelevant or at best tangential to qualifications for public office, and (3) news sources seldom made an issue of it, so there was no news "peg" that a reporter could use in reporting private indiscretions.

PRIVATE LIVES OF PUBLIC FIGURES

Public figures as news sources or news subjects have not objected to all news coverage of their private lives. In fact they have encouraged coverage of their private lives—on their own terms, which of course is their prerogative. Thus, a candidate's campaign literature and background information often is replete with pictures of the family, the family dog, family accomplishments. Aspects of the candidate's private life that would impress voters are thrust on the news media and the electorate.

Such insights into a person's private life may or may not be relevant to qualifications for public service or for celebrity. Even if favorable aspects of a private life are relevant, it does not automatically follow that indiscretions are relevant, too, or if relevant always harmful. For example, W. J. Cash said that early in this century Southerners preferred a candidate who was "a hell of a fellow," someone with a tinge of larceny or fast dealing, a blustery person who played by his own rules.[4] But once again it would be the public figure who would make and benefit from the disclosures—not the press.

Ambiguity abounds. Even after twenty-five or thirty years it is difficult to assess whether the administration of President John F. Kennedy, dubbed "Camelot" by the press, marked a change in the treatment of private lives of public figures or was just an aberration. Coverage was not given to President Kennedy's extramarital affairs—at least not at that time. But there was public fascination with the Kennedy clan, including questions about what brands of hand soap and toilet paper the family in the White House used!

For the most part, however, reporters agreed with news sources and news subjects that distinctions could be drawn between public and private lives. Issues of alcoholism and adultery were ignored by the press. Adultery was a problem between husband and wife, not between candidate and voter. A drunk could be a drunk in Congress or at a private bar so long as he was not arrested, in which case there would be a public record of the indiscretion, and the news story would not be based solely on a reporter's judgment to "invade" a public official's private life.

AN IRRELEVANT ISSUE

Reporters in the past often impersonated ostriches and put their heads in the sand when a public official misbehaved in a "private" way. The conventional wisdom among white, male news reporters and white, male public officials was that a private indiscretion was the official's own business so long as the act did not impinge on one's ability to carry out one's duties.

The irony in the understanding among reporters and between reporters and sources is that while all generally accepted the "duties" criterion, they also recognized that public charges of adultery would probably be a death knell at the polls. Voters would be unlikely to abide by the unwritten contract between reporters and public officials.

In essence, news reporters kept from the public information that would be important to many voters in electing government officials. Put in terms kinder to the reporter, the test for election or reelection was to be the candidate's public record or achievements in office and not his private life—even if the information about his private life would be important to many voters.

How far this logic was carried is evident in the life of Wendell Willkie, who ran for president against Franklin D. Roosevelt in 1940. The Republican Willkie was a dynamic, vibrant, charismatic public figure and also was a sort of informal bigamist—there was his wife, Edith, to whom he remained married until his death in October 1944, and Irita Van Doren, book editor for the *New York Herald Tribune* and a leader in New York literary circles, with whom Willkie had a loving relationship for several years. A Willkie biographer explains:

> Willkie's associates linked him with a variety of women ranging from secretaries to movie stars. "Willkie likes to play with a lot of women and is quite catholic in his tastes," Harold Ickes wrote privately. Gardner Cowles, Willkie's close friend, said, "He was not at all discreet. I thought it was careless and stupid." Willkie, though, told friends that his personal life was his own concern.[5]

Reporters and editors agreed with Willkie. Even in Mrs. Van Doren's obituary in the *New York Times*, December 19, 1966, the relationship with Willkie was dealt with by quoting a biographer who said, "In many ways, she was his closest friend."[6]

WHO IS THE SOURCE?

Reporters and editors were not likely to disclose a candidate's private indiscretions. But they probably would report about the indiscretions if another news source made an issue of it, shifting the subject from the private to the public arena.

The Democrats in 1940 knew about Willkie's affairs. Why didn't they disclose them? Partly because of the unwritten understanding of a distinction between public and private lives. Furthermore, Willkie's affairs would have provided handy ammunition for the Democrats if the Republicans had threatened to disclose private information about Roosevelt or his running mate, Henry Wallace. And that is what happened. Republicans came across some correspondence between Wallace and a White Russian mystic, letters that suggested Wallace had some odd religious beliefs and experiences. The Democrats let it be known that if the GOP went after Wallace, the Democrats would go after Willkie.[7] So voters in 1940 were left in the dark about two surefire issues: sex and religion.

In those days having a story that would be of interest to the news audience simply was not enough. The news reporter also needed a news source or a "news peg" to legitimize the story and to avoid criticism that the news reporter was invading someone's privacy. The news story thus became not that Willkie was an adulterer but that President Roosevelt said that Willkie was an adulterer.

The change in reporting practices in 1987 and 1988 was linked with sources and "news pegs." When Democrat Gary Hart was asked about sexual affairs, instead of saying it was a private matter, he invited the press to follow him. A government investigation turned up the marijuana use by Supreme Court nominee Douglas Ginsburg, and some presidential candidates acknowledged having smoked marijuana but said it happened long ago. Sources, at first anonymous, provided the press with a videotape documenting plagiarism by Sen. Joseph Biden, and Biden compounded his problems with inaccurate statements at a press conference.

Even if reporters sought to return to the "duties" criterion for deciding whether to report about the private lives of public figures, the nature of the 1987–88 news coverage has made it a more accepted practice for news sources to provide such information and make indiscretions campaign issues. The genie is out of the bottle.

NEW APPROACHES, OLD PROBLEMS

Criteria for news coverage of the private lives of public figures have changed. Nowadays separating private and public lives may be like trying to separate Siamese twins. In addition, topics for the public agenda have been liberalized. There may be some reversion, but the "duties" test has yielded to a "character" test — whether the private indiscretions reflect on a candidate's trustworthiness and reliability — and that test invites more, not less, coverage of private lives.

News coverage of Gary Hart and others was criticized not only because it was thought irrelevant to the issues but also because the focus on indiscretions came at the expense of other issues. News reporters hammered at the topic, almost setting a one-item agenda for covering Hart, which also affected coverage of other candidates. Having recognized that some information about a person's private life may be relevant to fitness for public office, one must also recognize that such information is only one part, perhaps a small part, of the electoral process.

What is healthy about the new approach is that voters — not reporters and not public officials — can decide whether information is important to them. To some, information about private lives will remain irrelevant; to others it can be a decisive factor. That is the way the system is supposed to work.

What is troubling is that the new-found latitude in reporting will exacerbate existing problems in news coverage. The news media are criticized for placing too much emphasis on the horse-race nature of a campaign and on campaign strategies, focusing on the style and mechanics of the process and not on substantive issues. A Peeping Tom mentality would only make things worse.

There is cause for optimism. First, public officials themselves can set some parameters on the coverage by simply refusing to comment when they consider questions inappropriate. Second, reactions from the news audience can help moderate the nature of coverage. These open approaches seem better ways to shape news coverage than old unwritten understandings between public officials and reporters.

Victims: public lives of private persons

Although the news audience is getting more information about the private lives of public figures, readers and viewers are probably getting less information about people involuntarily thrust into the news spotlight — even though such information often is a matter of public record. The almost universal practice of not identifying rape victims in news stories has been expanded so that the news media are more sensitive to questions about identifying victims of other crimes or printing addresses of victims or crime scenes.

Ralph Izard, director of the E. W. Scripps School of Journalism at Ohio University, reported:

> As a generalization, survey results indicate the media have evolved to a point in which they are willing to hold back on personal information which may be newsworthy but of limited significance when viewed in isolation.[8]

Noting that more than half of the broadcast and newspaper journalists who responded in the survey would be unlikely to use names *and* addresses of victims of routine burglaries, Izard wrote:

> The belief that making such information public may be dangerous, since burglaries often are repeated, or simply may be embarrassing, may have contributed to this response.

> Many respondents sought to overcome part of this concern by stipulating that they would use names [but] no addresses.[9]

Similar findings were reported in 1987 by faculty at Texas Christian University and Southern Methodist University in "The Right to Know vs. the Right to Privacy: Newspaper Identification of Crime Victims."[10]

Reasons for these changes in newsroom practices include societal concern with crime as a social and political issue and the forming of such agencies as the National Organization for Victim Assistance (NOVA), which symbolizes concern for helping citizens cope when they become victims of violence and crime. At best, such concerns encourage more responsible news coverage and provide news sources and news subjects more say in news stories about them. At worst, the reduction in news information may carry an insidious message that says in effect, "Look, our society is unable to deal with criminal activity. So, we'll do the next best thing: We won't tell anyone that you were a victim." Viewed in such a light, wrote Norbert Wiener, "This demand for secrecy is scarcely more than the wish of a sick civilization not to learn of [or to confront] the progress of its own disease."[11]

The best and the worst aspects provide the limits for the discussion of news coverage of private persons, which will be examined in the related terms of (1) privacy and dignity, (2) risks involved, and (3) newsroom responsibilities.

© King Features Syndicate, Inc., 1971. Reprinted with permission.

6

PRIVACY AND DIGNITY

To invoke the phrase "right of privacy" in discussions about identifying victims of crimes and other involuntary news sources can be misleading. Protection of privacy in the form of nondisclosure of a victim's name and address is, for practical purposes, a newsroom decision, not a courtroom decision. In instances of outrageous press behavior a victim may have legal recourse against a newspaper or a broadcast station, but the record of a crime is a public record. News coverage of information in that public record tells the news audience what is happening in their community, whom it is happening to, and what, if anything, public servants are doing about it. Invoking the phrase "right of privacy" also can be misleading because a victim usually is not seeking legal recourse. The victim seeks a responsible, compassionate, and sensitive community response — a response that generally is more in the hands of neighbors and news reporters than in the hands of a judge.

David A. Anderson, a professor of law at the University of Texas, noted, however, that victims do have some control over the nature of news coverage:

> You don't have to give interviews. . . . You don't have to allow the press to come on your property — into your home or office, even if it is the scene of the crime. . . . You don't have to let yourself be used by the police or prosecutor. They have a continuing relationship with the press and they may be more eager than you are to publicize your case.
>
> [Although] the bottom line is that the courts are not very likely to protect a crime victim from unwanted publicity . . . [v]ictims do have privacy rights. But those rights are less likely to be vindicated by legal remedies than by other means: by victims knowing how to look out for themselves, by persuading the press to observe some common decency and humanity in dealing with crime victims, and by sensitizing police and prosecutors to the needs of victims.[12]

Suggestions for coverage. The difficulty in placing much of a burden upon the victim as news source is that the person is likely to be so traumatized by an act of violence that coping with the news media only multiplies the problems. Still, there is a need for both the news source and the news reporter to have an understanding of their relationship. The National Organization for Victim Assistance, as an intervenor, gives this advice to news reporters:

> Provide the public with factual, objective information about crime stories. . . . Present a balanced view of crime by ensuring that the victim and the criminal perspective are given equal coverage when possible. . . . When reporting conversations with victims, quote victims, families, and friends fairly and in context. . . . [Do not] print or broadcast unverified or ambiguous facts about the victim, his/her demeanor, background or relationships to the offender . . . [or] print or broadcast facts about the crime, the victim, or the criminal act that might embarrass, humiliate, hurt or upset the victim unless there is a need to publish such details for public safety reasons.[13]

Such guidelines do not so much offer a blueprint for news coverage — publishing information "for public safety reasons" provides considerable latitude — as they suggest that reporters reflect upon the nature of news coverage and not merely react to events.

Persons with disabilities. Crime victims are not the only private persons troubled by the nature of public attention. People with disabilities and the mentally ill and their families also are concerned that their situations be better understood by the press and public. Often it is a matter of the language used in a story. For example, here are some recommended word usages for reporting on people with disabilities, developed by free-lance writer William L. Rush, a graduate of the University of Nebraska School of Journalism:

> *Confined* — People with disabilities are no more "confined to a wheelchair" than people with poor vision are "confined to their glasses." Try "uses a wheelchair for mobility" or "gets around by wheelchair."

Disabled person — Try "person with a disability," thus putting the person before the disability.

Handicap — Do not use to describe a person's physical condition. Persons with disabilities are not necessarily handicapped. The term *handicap* refers to environmental barriers preventing or making it difficult for full participation or integration.

Victim — A person with a disability was not sabotaged, nor was the individual necessarily in a car, plane, or train accident. Having a disability need not make a person a victim.

Rush also offers suggestions for interviewing people with disabilities:

Remember that a person with a disability is a person like anyone else. Never mind if the person can't extend a hand for a handshake. Personal contact is still important.

Relax. If you don't know what to say or do, let the person who has the disability help put you at ease.

Speak directly to a person with a disability. Don't assume a companion or assistant to be a conversational go-between.

If you are talking to a person . . . through a sign language interpreter, speak directly to the person. . . . Do not say: "Ask him/her what his/her name is." Say: "What is your name."

Divide the interview into two parts and ask questions about (I) the disability, and (II) other subjects. Before the interview decide what part is more important. For example, if interviewing a political leader with a disability about . . . foreign affairs, [the] disability is irrelevant. But if you're interviewing the same politician about . . . national health insurance, the disability may be important.[14]

Other insights into sensitive areas of news coverage may come after the fact. Reporters who use a medical term like "schizophrenia" flippantly — such as saying a football coach is schizophrenic about which quarterback to start — are likely to get a phone call or a letter cautioning them about such inaccurate usage. That is because support groups and others are speaking out on behalf of persons with mental illness and their families. This response helps make for a healthier society and for better-informed reporters.

Reporting causes of death.   Even as recently as the 1960s much of the press reported that people died of one of two causes: a long illness or a short illness. About the only clue to the actual cause of death was a notice that the family requested contributions be made to the American Cancer Society or the American Heart Association. The logic, in part, was that it might be embarrassing to have died of cancer or that listing cancer as a cause of death just recalled the deceased's suffering. It was also argued that the cause of death was a private matter and need not be shared with strangers in the news audience.

Newspapers have become more open in reporting causes of death, and the "long illness" or "short illness" ambiguity has disappeared from many obituary pages. After all, there is nothing embarrassing or humiliating about dying. Everyone will. Furthermore, listing the causes of death may make readers more sensitive to health care issues and also is consistent with the ground rules of this chapter, such as the latitude of the First Amendment and the preference for openness.

Because of the community orientation of most newspapers, however, editors and reporters remain sensitive to family concerns in listing a cause of death. As a result, they seldom run a detailed account of the illness. Deaths from, say, alcoholism might be listed as having been caused by a liver ailment.

This news process can be illustrated by an episode in which the family refused to tell a reporter the cause of death of a 29-year-old man who died out of town. Getting the cause of death was easy enough: the reporter simply phoned the coroner's office in the distant city. The man had died in a drunken seizure by banging his head against the bars of his jail cell. A young reporter, eager to demonstrate the power of the free press, was ready to put that information into an obituary. He conferred with an assistant city editor. The decision was made to abide by the family's wishes and not print the specific cause of death.

Why? First of all, many reporting discussions in a newsroom are made in this fashion; a reporter confronting an ethical decision should take advantage of insights from colleagues. In this case the assistant city editor reasoned that (1) the family's wish should be honored because there was no compelling community interest in the case, particularly since the death had occurred elsewhere (although a newspaper in the community in which the death occurred would likely be concerned about a death in a public facility); (2) the newspaper would have shirked its duties had it not gotten the full information, and now, having all the information, the paper could make an informed judgment about what to print; and (3) the man probably had caused the family enough grief in his life – why add to it by reporting the cause of his death? This final reason is based on an unfounded, subjective judgment by the editor.

This episode is an example of what journalists mean by addressing issues on a case-by-case basis. Such decisions might be inconsistent or unpredictable – even contradictory and wrong at times – but the process does seek to weigh newsroom priorities against the concerns of news sources and news subjects. In this case the paper may have decided too readily that it was the responsibility of someone else to cover a death in a public facility; such news should not be a matter of county lines.

Suicide. A decision whether to report that a person committed suicide generally is made by the county coroner or medical examiner. If that public official lists suicide as the cause of death, it generally will be reported as such. Because of the reliance on official sources, the number of suicides in the nation is greater than statistics suggest. How can one always know if an overdose of some medication was taken purposely or if a gun discharged accidentally? Furthermore, a coroner mindful of family concerns might report that "an autopsy is pending" to determine cause of death – a maneuver that at least keeps the suicide report out of the next day's obituary page. For religious reasons or insurance purposes a family might wish that a death not be listed as a suicide if there are other possible explanations, and this might weigh on the coroner's mind. (The official, of course, cannot take part in an insurance fraud.) Traffic fatalities, too, may include a share of suicides.

If the apparent suicide or suicide attempt is made in a public fashion—by jumping off a building, for example—or involves a public figure, then other news concerns enter the equation, and the news media will pursue the story and provide the news audience with more information than would normally be the case.

AIDS-related deaths. Another recent issue in news reporting is whether AIDS (acquired immune deficiency syndrome) should be linked with the cause of death because of the connotation of homosexual activity, drug addiction, or promiscuity. Arthur L. Caplan, director of the Center of Biomedical Ethics at the University of Minnesota, noted that it is important for society to know the impact of AIDS in order to assess health care needs, conduct research, and determine spending for prevention and treatment of the disease. Then why are physicians reluctant to report AIDS as related to the cause of death?

> The answer is quite simple. The primary moral responsibility of a physician is not to the state, the government, the department of health, or to those groups most vulnerable to AIDS. It is to the patients in his or her care. . . . Physicians must assure those who seek their care that they will do all they can to maintain the sanctity of the doctor-patient relationship. . . .
> The mentally ill, rape victims, the chemically dependent, and many other vulnerable members of society may be reluctant to seek medical care if they do not believe their privacy will be protected.
> . . . Physicians must do what they can to protect privacy because they are obligated to try to maintain the autonomy and freedom of patients despite the presence of disease. The dying have precious few choices left to them in life. One of the few matters they can control is what is publicly known about the manner and cause of their dying.[15]

But do the dying forfeit control over reporting their cause of death because of a compelling public interest in knowing the scope and treatment of a communicable disease? The news media began more frequent reporting of AIDS-related deaths because (1) the deaths were one sign of the widespread nature of the epidemic; (2) in some cases no objections were raised by the family, the victim's illness had already been reported, or he or she had requested that the cause of death be listed; and (3) if AIDS resulted from a blood transfusion or was otherwise not sexually transmitted, that fact could be noted in the press. Eventually public notice of AIDS could no longer be avoided, as it moved to the schoolyard and claimed the lives of third and fourth graders who had been treated for hemophilia. Furthermore, gay rights groups have helped move issues of homosexuality into the public forum and have lessened the ostracism of homosexuals. But still a family's direct request to a newspaper not to link AIDS with the cause of death may persuade an editor to withhold the information, particularly if the paper routinely abides by family wishes in obituaries.

At least the question of how to handle AIDS-related deaths in obituaries can theoretically be resolved more easily in the 1980s than it might have been in the 1960s. State laws often do provide for some privacy for persons with communicable diseases. A person who reports to a county health clinic to be tested for gonorrhea or syphilis may be assured that the record of the test will be confidential. In this instance the judgment is that it is more important that people be treated for venereal disease than for society at large to know the names of persons treated. The confidential records are available to health care officials only. Keeping a cause of death confidential, however, is a different problem. Saying that the cause of death is "confidential" is tantamount to saying the death resulted from AIDS or another stigmatized disease. Other issues arise, too, and Caplan's concerns will continue to be part of the AIDS debate.

U.S. Rep. Stewart McKinney, a Connecticut Republican, died of AIDS-related illness in May 1987, the first congressman known to have so died. His physician said that McKinney probably contracted AIDS from blood transfusions received during heart bypass surgery in 1979. The *Washington Post*, however, reported that anonymous sources disclosed that the nine-term congressman might have caught AIDS through homosexual activity. The *Post* defended their report on the grounds that their information came from "sources whose identity and credibility are well known to us." The few AIDS-related deaths attributed to blood transfusions—about 2 percent—also called into question the physician's explanation. The *Post* was criticized for using anonymous sources and for being preoccupied with the cause of McKinney's death instead of with his fine record as a congressman.

If a private, less prominent citizen were an AIDS victim and a physician said the death resulted from a blood transfusion, a local newspaper would be acting responsibly in calling that explanation into question if it had reliable, on-the-record information to the contrary. Use of anonymous sources in a case such as this might be warranted to allay public concerns about the community blood supply. But under a rigorous test linking use of anonymous sources with the publication of information of vital interest to the public, it is difficult to justify the anonymity the *Post* provided in the McKinney case.

Whether the deceased be a congressman or a private citizen, the individual's contributions to society should not be lost sight of in the controversy over the cause of death. There needs to be some faith in an informed citizenry's ability to make sound judgments.

The space shuttle *Challenger* disaster.   For much of the rest of this century discussions about the restraint of the press and the need for dignity in reporting will include an examination of news coverage of the explosion of the space shuttle *Challenger* and the televised deaths of seven astronauts on January 28, 1986. Mike Pride, editor of the *Concord* (N.H.) *Monitor* wrote of how the news media descended on his city, home of the teacher-astronaut Christa McAuliffe. He noted how repulsive the behavior of some journalists was and yet how the coverage was important. Here is what he said about a memorial mass:

> Before the Mass at St. John's began, the Rev. Dan Messier . . . descended from the sanctuary to comfort a young boy in the front pew. It was as though a single duck

had flown into a blind occupied by 50 hunters. Rapid-fire clicks and flashes zeroed in on the scene as the boy buried his head in Messier's shoulder.

Pride wrote of other distractions created by the journalists and added:

> I had gone to St. John's to confront my own feelings about what had happened, and I left without having done so. The media were the reason. The priests could have kept the media out or allowed only a pool in. I wish they had, even though I see the other side of the issue.
>
> Messier saw both sides too. He talked to his congregation about it the next Sunday. The media had behaved badly, he said, but since the pictures of that Mass and an earlier service for children appeared on television, he had had calls from everywhere. The whole country felt a bond with the grieving people of Concord.[16]

A measure of dignity survived despite the news media coverage. Reverend Messier was kind not to point out that the bond with Concord might have been established just as well if the news media had covered the service in less obtrusive fashion, perhaps through a pool, as Pride suggested. One guideline for coverage in such circumstances is that news reporters, camera crews, and photographers should respond as though covering a death within the family — as, in a sense, all deaths are.

THE RISKS INVOLVED

The "risks" argument for not disclosing information about an involuntary news source or news subject — because of the harm such disclosure might cause — has a dubious distinction: it probably is the most common argument put forward by news sources and victims. It also is the least persuasive argument in the newsroom — at least in theory. News media are asked not to report the address of a home that has been burglarized for fear the burglars will return; or they are asked to not print the name of a holdup victim for fear the gunman will strike again; or other information is not reported in order to save the victim further embarrassment or suffering. The NOVA guidelines suggest restraint in reporting information that "might embarrass, humiliate, hurt or upset the victim unless there is a need to publish such details for public safety reasons." That is casting a rather wide net.

The "risks" approach to routine news reporting is unpersuasive for at least five reasons:

1. There should be nothing embarrassing or humiliating about being the victim of a burglary, holdup, or other crime. If there is a wrongful stigma attached to being the victim of a crime, that stigma may only be reinforced if information about the crime is not published. The news media in essence would send the signal that it is so shameful to be victimized that even they, the news media, avert their eyes; meanwhile other members of society cannot offer support because they are not informed.

2. Nondisclosure has risks of its own. If a crime is reported in a neighborhood, residents should know about it in order to take whatever safety measures they wish. "Why didn't someone tell me?" is a reasonable complaint from a second victim.

3. The "risks" approach contradicts most of the ground rules discussed earlier by giving a preference to secrecy over openness.

4. In most cases the identity of the victim—name and address—is known, has been learned, or can be ascertained readily by the criminal. If the intent of nondisclosure is to protect the victim from a second assault, such nondisclosure provides a false sense of security at best.

5. Specific names and addresses add credibility and substance to the report of a crime. Criminal acts hurt specific people, not a faceless and nameless 37-year-old man. Crimes occur in specific locations, not in a generalized 3400 block of Melanie Drive. Covering crime news in anonymous and secretive fashion does little to alert citizens to the impact or extent of criminal activity. Similarly, reluctance of the news media to be specific in reporting cases of child and spouse abuse (because such abuse was defined as a domestic matter or because it was feared reporting the abuse would

threaten the innocent victims) helped cover up the magnitude of a serious social problem.

Despite these reasons, the "risks" argument is a popular one. Why? Because the fears are legitimate to the people involved, and perhaps because such an argument is effective often enough. Reporters and editors can add to the reasons for not keeping things secret. They still do so on a case-by-case basis, as the Ohio University and TCU/SMU research suggests. The news media are sensitive to the victim's fears — real or imagined.

NEWSROOM RESPONSIBILITIES

Journalists cannot save the world; they cannot even lessen the grief of a mother and father whose son was killed in a traffic accident. What journalists can do is to be accurate, comprehensive, informed, and sensitive in their news reporting. And in reporting on those thrust into the news spotlight, journalists can be objective — not objective in the sense of detached or impartial, but objective in the sense that social psychologist Erich Fromm used the word, which was in terms of *respect*. Just as a journalist treats a point of view with respect in news reporting, so the journalist can respect the conditions and predicaments of news sources. The curious thing about such an approach to reporting is that, like preparation, it pays dividends for the reporter, the news source, and the audience.

Sympathy comes easy. Nick Lamberto, after more than forty years as a reporter with the *Des Moines Register,* still intrigued young reporters with his ability to get information from reluctant news sources. A newsroom desk next to his was coveted because it offered a program of continuing education. At least three of his ground rules were these: never lie to a news source, never use anonymous sources, and in situations of grief and trauma, "You've got to be sympathetic. That's not hard to do." One key to Lamberto's success was to define himself as a helper in the eyes of the news source: "You don't want to talk to all the reporters? You don't have to; just talk with me." "You're upset with what reporters have been writing? Well, let's talk and perhaps I can help get your story across." Or he might say, "I know this is a trying time for your family. But it would help if you'd share a little information with me, so I can be sure our story is accurate."

Lamberto knew what other reporters learn: in times of grief people may find it helpful, almost therapeutic, to talk. Surprisingly, many even feel a sense of support in that the local newspaper or broadcast station cares enough to seek information, particularly if they are approached in a sympathetic manner.

The point is not that Lamberto and other skilled reporters covet such assignments or that they are valued because they can extract personal information from grieving news sources before the sources "know what hit 'em." To the contrary, reporters who readily volunteer for such assignments should be suspect. As the ground rules for this chapter explain, there are appropriate reasons for a Nick Lamberto to make a phone call or a visit to those in grief.

If that is so and if information useful to the news audience results from such thoughtful approaches to the news source, why are reporters often characterized as ghouls and vultures? In some situations news reporters will be characterized as ghouls, regardless of any mitigating efforts. The newsroom judgment will be to report what a source does not want reported or to cover an action that the source regrets having taken. In such instances the reporter focuses on the accuracy of the story, seeking appropriate comment from the news source. Furthermore, as Roy Peter Clark, who has worked with newspapers across the nation as a writing coach, observed, the reporter may have more options than simply disclosure or nondisclosure:

> In any given situation the decision may be among a dozen possible alternatives. Publish it right away; don't publish at all; publish at a later date. Publish a picture boldly on page one; crop it; use it inside the paper. Show the dead body; show the chalk outline on the sidewalk; show the body bag; show a grieving family member; feature the police. These choices are

not the mere exercise of journalistic craft. Each choice is loaded with ethical ramifications.[17]

Obstacles to sensitive reporting. Any of these options may be upsetting to the news source or audience. Obstacles to sensitive reporting, however, are not found in thoughtful consideration of options but in such areas as might be termed pack journalism, transmission-belt journalism, and callous journalism.

Pack journalism: Clark summarized the problems here well:

> As individuals reporters can take advantage of their humanity, suffer with the victim, participate in and facilitate a process of catharsis and grief, and help give public meaning to the life of the victim. The problem occurs when the journalist becomes part of an anonymous and rapacious group. . . . It is the public vision of the voracious, unfeeling pack that dehumanizes us, hurts victims, and makes us so unpopular.[18]

Just add cameras, flash bulbs, television cable, microphones, and other reporting paraphernalia to the news-reporting pack, and it becomes even easier to understand why such behavior is interpreted to be uncaring and ruthless.

Transmission-belt journalism: Some news reporters may resolve an ethical problem in terms of possession of the information. If you have it, print it; if you've taped it, air it.

We return to the coverage of R. Budd Dwyer, considered briefly in this chapter's discussion of the nature of the news media. Dwyer, a state official in Pennsylvania, killed himself at a press conference by placing the barrel of a .357 Magnum in his mouth and pulling the trigger. His death was recorded on videotape and in still photographs. Some stations aired the footage of the scene, warning viewers ahead of time in case they did not want to see a man's head blown away. Some newspapers ran a still photo in which remnants of the back of Dwyer's skull gave him a gory halo.

To what end? For what purpose? The death was amply documented; there was no question about how he died. There was little doubt about the outcome of placing a powerful handgun in one's mouth and pulling the trigger. In broadcasting and publishing the death scene, some news media forgot that possession of the information is what creates the problem in the first place, not what solves it.

Callous journalism: People who deal with tragedy on almost a daily basis need some defense mechanisms. Nurses who work in a ward for terminally ill children develop loving relationships with their patients but cannot allow themselves to be emotionally shattered each time one dies, otherwise they would be of little help to other patients. Social workers cannot carry the psychological and financial burdens of each of one hundred or more families in their caseloads. If they do, such concern becomes dysfunctional and the person obsessed with helping becomes unable to help. Likewise, journalists cannot get so caught up in the tragedy of a family that they are unable to share information with the news audience.

In order to cope, one needs to find ways to deal with the daily tragedies. That is one reason for so-called sick humor in many professions and perhaps, in some cases, for high rates of alcoholism. To cope in a successful and healthy fashion, one may develop a philosophy that recognizes and cherishes the frailty of life and accepts, as best one can, the quirks, flukes, and accidents that often determine when one suffers or dies. And rather than resorting to a *que sera sera* philosophy, one recognizes the great opportunity of having a job that can make a difference in society. The risk is that a person—in our context a journalist—is or becomes so callous that he or she dehumanizes others, figuring that is the only way get the work done and to be productive in covering news of grief.

Justified intrusions.   Jeff Greenfield, a political and media analyst for ABC News, has spoken to such concerns about the dehumanizing aspects of journalism:

> We . . . need to acknowledge something about the way journalists behave when they confront human beings under enormous pain and grief. And that is that we often respond "pro-

fessionally" — and I mean that in the worst possible sense of that word. . . .

But, of course, journalists would not excuse other people for behaving callously. They would run exposes, demand to know why these people hadn't been given sensitivity training. That's not a bad question to ask of ourselves: why can't we behave in a more civilized manner when doing our jobs — even if that does sound "weak" or "prissy?" . . .

Once we put those admissions on the table, however, we are left with the tougher issue: why have we — people in the business of communications — done so bad a job of explaining why intrusion into people's private lives is in fact often justified — or even required of us? . . . If there's an issue of propriety, a note to the readers or viewers may help convince them that you're not simply in the business of selling more papers or getting higher ratings. Explaining our actions seems to me one important, much neglected step in playing it straight with our clients.[19]

As an illustration of "openness," Greenfield noted that the *Wall Street Journal* explained to readers why it ran a lengthy story about the chronic spouse abuse committed by the head of the enforcement division of the Securities and Exchange Commission.

Greenfield's point is that while the news media may assume it is their First Amendment right, if not their duty, to cover controversial stories, readers and viewers might not agree. Therefore, an explanation such as that provided by the *Wall Street Journal* — or in other cases by newspaper ombudsmen, "readers' representatives," and other media representatives — can serve two purposes: such information may help the news audience understand the news process, and such a practice can remind the news medium, as well, about the risks of pack journalism, transmission-belt journalism, and callous journalism.

Summary

News sources include those persons involuntarily thrust into the public spotlight, whether because they are public officials whose private lives come under scrutiny or because they are victims of crime or other social ills. Although the resulting news coverage often is criticized, reasons for such reporting include the latitude of the First Amendment and a system of government that gives a decided preference to openness and information over secrecy.

News coverage of the private lives of public officials has changed. Historically distinctions were drawn between an official's public and private lives, and private indiscretions were not reported unless the private conduct might impinge on public duties or there was some incident such as an arrest to provide a reason for reporting on the official's private life. In recent years, however, the "duties" test has given way to a "character" test; conduct in one's private life has come to be viewed as a relevant measure of one's trustworthiness and reliability. It is likely that in the future there will be less distinction between the public and private lives of news sources and news subjects.

Newsrooms may be reporting more about the private lives of public officials, but some research suggests that these same newsrooms are becoming more sensitive to the concerns of crime victims and other involuntary news sources and news subjects. Such people have a limited legal right to privacy when it comes to reporting about them, but the ethical concerns involved are provocative. Reporters are learning to be more sensitive in reporting about persons with disabilities, for example, and in dealing with situations of grief and trauma.

Some argue that news coverage of crime victims may place them in greater jeopardy, but such "risk" arguments, although popular, generally are flawed. Rather than argue about the risks involved, it seems the wiser course to work toward accurate, informed, comprehensive, and sensitive news reporting that accords news sources appropriate respect.

Even with respectful reporting it is likely that some will still consider reporters ghouls, but reporters do little to change that picture if they resort to forms of reporting that dehumanize both the news source and the news reporter.

It is appropriate to conclude this section with a quote from sociologist Robert Park, who wrote about "The Natural History of the Newspaper" and news reporting in the *American Journal of Sociology* in November 1923. His observations about the human nature of the news media still have merit today and are applicable to the broadcast media as well:

> What then is the remedy for the existing condition of the newspaper? There is no remedy. Humanly speaking, the present newspapers are about as good as they can be. If the newspapers are to be improved, it will come through the education of the people and the organization of political information and intelligence. . . .
>
> The real reason that the ordinary newspaper accounts of the incidents of ordinary life are so sensational is because we know so little of human life that we are not able to interpret the events of life when we read them.

Notes

Chapter 1

1. The concept provided the basis of *The Fourth Branch of Government* by Douglass Cater (Random House, New York, 1965).

2. John Lancaster wrote of his unforeseen travails as a witness in "Woodstein in Des Moines: Memoirs of a Reporter Who Hoped to Change the World," *Columbia Journalism Review*, Jan./Feb. 1983, pp.51–52. He was summoned to testify about news stories dealing with the laxity of city rental-housing inspectors.

3. Jay Hamburg, "Bakker Falls from Grace but His Park Carries On," *Orlando Sentinel*, Mar. 27, 1987, pp.A-1 and A-6.

4. Ibid.

5. Mitch Coleman, in "A Day in the Life" (*The Quill*, July/Aug. 1983, pp. 22–23), tells how such an experience helped drive him from journalism. His call to the wife of a murder victim was wrongly interpreted by other news media and the police, who castigated him as thoughtless and callous for seeking a reaction from the distraught woman when he told her the news in sympathetic fashion and generally followed the procedures suggested in this chapter.

6. John Weisman, "Betrayal and Trust: The Tricky Art of Finding – and Keeping – Good TV News Sources," *TV Guide*, Mar. 7–13, 1987.

7. The First Amendment to the U.S. Constitution reads: "Congress shall make no law respecting an establishment of religion, or prohibiting the free exercise thereof; or abridging the freedom of speech, or of the press, or the right of the people peaceably to assemble, and to petition the Government for a redress of grievances."

8. Dan Thomasson, "Cheap-shot Journalism," *The Quill*, Jan. 1986, p.18.

9. Warren Strugatch, "The C-word Produces Queasy Moments in the Newsroom," *The Quill*, Dec. 1987, pp.14–15.

10. Madelyn S. Gould and David Shaffer, "The Impact of Suicide in Television Movies: Evidence of Imitation," *New England Journal of Medicine,* Sept. 11, 1986, pp.690–96.

11. Turner Catledge, *My Life and The Times* (Harper & Row, New York, 1971), p.264.

Chapter 2

1. Dick Haws, an associate professor of journalism at Iowa State University, discussed the faulty U.S. reporting in "Fallout from U.S. Media's Coverage of Chernobyl: Exaggeration, Sloppiness, Blind Reliance on 'Sources,' " in the *Des Moines Register,* July 25, 1986, p.13A.

2. John Weisman, "Betrayal and Trust: The Tricky Art of Finding—and Keeping—Good TV News Sources," *TV Guide*, Mar. 7–13, 1987.

3. An excellent reading on this topic is *Lying: Moral Choice in Public and Private Life* by Sissela Bok (Pantheon Books, New York, 1978).

4. Walter Lippmann, "Stereotypes," in *Public Opinion* (Free Press, New York, 1965), pp.54–55.

5. Bill Moyers, "God and Politics: The Kingdom Divided," Public Affairs Television, Inc., Dec. 9, 1987.

6. Jack Perkins, "The Mind of an Assassin," *First Tuesday*, NBC News, June 3, 1969.

7. The YIPPIES were members of the self–proclaimed Youth International Party, who manipulated the media and helped the Chicago and Democratic party establishment "freak out" with proposals to drop LSD into the city's water supply, paint their cars like cabs and take convention delegates to Wisconsin, and use black widow spiders to attack police. Many of the proposals were reported in straightforward fashion by the news media.

8. Quoted in Anthony Marro, "When the Government Tells Lies," *Columbia Journalism Review,* Mar./Apr. 1985, p.36.

9. Ibid., p.38.

10. The program, "American Vice: The Doping of a Nation," was broadcast Dec. 2, 1986. Rosenberg's commentary, "Rivera's Vice: Duping of a Nation," appeared in the *Des Moines Register*, Dec. 5, 1986.

11. Leon V. Sigal, *Reporters and Officials: The Organization and Politics of Newsmaking*, (D.C. Heath and Co., Lexington, Mass., 1973), p.7, from a panel discussion at the Institute of Politics, Kennedy School of Government, Harvard University, May 19, 1970.

12. Telephone interview with James McCartney when he was city editor of the *Chicago Daily News*, May 6, 1968.

13. Jules Witcover, *White Knight: The Rise of Spiro Agnew* (Random House, New York, 1972), p.364.

Chapter 3

1. "The Case of the Plastic Peril," *CBS Reports*, Oct. 19, 1974.

2. Sam Donaldson, *Hold on, Mr. President!* (Random House, New York, 1987), pp.18–19.

3. Donald Kaul, *The End of the World As We Know It* (Image and Idea, Iowa City, 1979), p.4.

4. Eugene J. Webb and Jerry R. Salancik, *The Interview, or The Only Wheel in Town,* Journalism Monograph No. 2, Association for Education in Journalism, Austin, Texas, Nov. 1966; Eugene J. Webb et al., *Unobtrusive Measures: Nonreactive Research in the Social Sciences* (Rand McNally, Chicago, 1966).

5. *New York Times*, Jan. 26, 1988, p.1.

6. "Controversial Comments," *Wall Street Week,* program no. 435, Mar. 28, 1975, Maryland Center for Public Broadcasting, Baltimore.

7. Wendell Rawls, Jr., "Interviewing: The Crafty Art," *Columbia Journalism Review*, Nov./Dec. 1982, p.47.

8. Mitchell Stephens and Eliot Frankel, "The Counterpunch Interview," *Columbia Journalism Review*, Mar./Apr. 1983, p.38.

9. Robert Hullihan, "Finally, Our Man Asks Tough Questions," *Des Moines Register*, Aug. 15, 1976, p.1A.

10. Webb and Salancik, *The Interview*, p.21.

11. Ibid., p.30.

12. A. J. Liebling, *The Most of A. J. Liebling* (Simon and Schuster, New York, 1963), p.157.

13. Halina J. Czerniejewski, "Guidelines," *The Quill*, July/Aug. 1977, p.21.

Chapter 4

1. Ben Hecht, *Gaily, Gaily: The Memoirs of a Cub Reporter in Chicago* (Doubleday, New York, 1963), p.226.

2. Donald McDonald, "Memoranda to Center Members," *The Center Magazine,* Mar./Apr. 1987, vol.20, no.2, p.3.

3. William L. Rivers, *The Adversaries* (Beacon Books, Boston, 1970), p. 69.

4. Hecht, *Gaily, Gaily,* p.2.

5. Murray Kempton, "Casey and Woodward: Who Used Whom?" *New York Review of Books*, Nov. 5, 1987, p. 61. See also Thomas Powers, "How Casey Wooed Woodward," *New York Review of Books,* Nov. 19, 1987, pp.8–11.

6. Richard Scott Mowrer, "The Press Is in Danger of Manipulation When It Quotes Anonymous Sources," *presstime*, June 1987, p.74.

7. Michael Gartner, comments in a panel discussion at a meeting of the Associated Press Managing Editors association in Seattle, Sept. 18, 1987.

8. Ibid.

9. *Minneapolis Tribune* staff memo no.54, Sept. 19, 1969.

10. Steve Ronald, personal correspondence with author, Dec. 19, 1987.

11. New York Times Co. v. Sullivan, 376 U.S. 254 (1964), p. 270.

12. Ronald, personal correspondence, Dec. 19, 1987.

13. Quoted in an Associated Press story of October 10, 1976.

14. The Madison, Wis., *Capital Times* reported the full quote, as did the Toledo, Ohio, *Blade*. The *Blade* decided to do so only after Butz had resigned, since the remarks "may affect the outcome of the election and therefore the future of the country." President Gerald Ford was defeated by Jimmy Carter in the 1976 election, but the Butz comment was not viewed as decisive.

15. Clark R. Mollenhoff, *Game Plan for Disaster* (Norton, New York, 1976), p.66.

16. Ibid., p.72.

17. "Navy Whistle Blower, Frustrated and Angry, Resigns," June 18, 1987, copyright by the *Dallas Morning News*, reported in the *Des Moines Register*.

18. Randy Evans, "Nuclear Plant Guard Bitter after Exposé," *Des Moines Register*, Feb. 18, 1979, p.1B.

19. "Newsmakers," *Newsweek*, Feb. 8, 1988, p.78.

20. See, for example, Lamberto v. Brown, Iowa. 326 N.W. 2d 305, Nov. 24, 1982.

21. Leonard W. Levy, *Freedom of Speech and Press in Early American History: Legacy of Suppression* (Harper and Row, New York, 1963) pp.287–88. A similar passage is found in Levy's *Emergence of a Free Press* (Oxford University Press, New York, 1985), pp.330–31, a revision of the 1963 work. The *Legacy* quote is preferred here partly because of its reference to a "pernicious silence"; also,

Wortman's phrase "imbecility of understanding" has some nineteenth–century charm.

22. Rosato V. Superior Court, App., 124 *Cal. Reporter* 427.

23. "Two Leaks, But by Whom? North's Charges against Congress Have Some Holes," *Newsweek*, July 27, 1987, p.16.

24. "Breaking a Confidence: When Is It Right to Reveal an Anonymous Source?" *Time*, Aug. 3, 1987, p.61.

25. Paul Lazarsfeld and Robert Merton, "Mass Communication, Popular Taste and Organized Social Action," *Readings in Social Psychology*, rev. ed. (Holt, New York, 1952), p.76

Chapter 5

1. Cal Thomas, "Not Ready for Prime-time Prayers," *The Quill,* Oct. 1986, p.16.

2. Judy VanSlyke Turk, *Information Subsidies and Media Content: A Study of Public Relations Influence on the News,* Journalism Monographs, no. 100, Association for Education in Journalism and Mass Communication, Columbia, S.C., Dec. 1986.

3. Ibid., p.13.

4. Ibid., p.22.

5. Julius Duscha, "Nader's Raiders Put the Washington Press Corps to Shame," *The Progressive*, Apr. 1971, pp.24–26.

6. Harold C. Relyea, "USFOIA Faces Technology Challenges," *Transnational Data and Communications Report (TDR)*, vol. 10, no. 6, June 1987, pp.15–17.

7. Evan Hendricks, *Former Secrets* (Campaign for Political Rights, 201 Massachusetts Avenue NE, Washington, DC, 20002, 1982).

8. *New York Times*, Apr. 29, 1985, p.A17.

9. Hans Linde, "Advice to the Press," *Center Magazine*, Jan./Feb. 1979, p.5.

10. Michael Moss, "The Poverty Story," *Columbia Journalism Review*, July/ Aug. 1987, p.52.

11. Philip Meyer, *Precision Journalism* (Indiana University Press, Bloomington, 1973), pp.14–15.

12. Maxwell McCombs, Donald Lewis Shaw, and David Grey, *Handbook of Reporting Methods* (Houghton Mifflin, Boston, 1976), p.ix.

13. Commission on Freedom of the Press, *A Free and Responsible Press* (University of Chicago Press, Chicago, 1963), p.26. The Commission's report was first issued in 1947.

14. Tom Wicker, "The Reporter and His Story: How Far Should He Go," *Nieman Reports,* Sept. 1972, pp.15–17.

15. Michael Moss, "The Poverty Story," p.43.

16. Ibid., p.47.

17. Ibid., p.54.

18. Ibid.

19. L. John Martin, "The Media's Role in International Terrorism," *Terrorism: An International Journal*, vol. 8, no. 2, 1985, p.130.

20. Quoted in David Shaw, "Editors Face Terrorist Demand Dilemma," *Los Angeles Times*, Sept. 15, 1976.

21. A good account of the Hanafi Muslim episode was written by one of the hostages, Charles Fenyvesi, "Looking into the Muzzle of Terrorists," *The Quill*, July/Aug. 1977, pp.16–18.

22. Ibid., p.16–17.

23. I am grateful to graduate student Steve Salato for making available for use here his research paper, "The First Amendment and Terrorism: Coverage of the 1985 TWA Hijacking."

24. Edwin Diamond, "The Coverage Itself—Why It Turned into 'Terrorvision,' " *TV Guide,* Sept. 21, 1985.

25. Michael J. O'Neill, *Terrorist Spectaculars: Should TV Coverage Be Curbed?* (Priority Press Publications, New York, 1986), p.6.

26. Diamond, "The Coverage Itself," p.13.

27. O'Neill, "Terrorist Spectaculars," p.52.

28. Ibid., p.103.

29. John Merrill is the author of two works on the importance of journalistic integrity: *The Imperative of Freedom: A Philosophy of Journalistic Autonomy,* 1974, and *Existential Journalism,* 1977, both published by Hastings House, New York.

Chapter 6

1. Charles Fenyvesi, "Looking into the Muzzle of Terrorists," *The Quill*, July/Aug. 1977, p.17.

2. Eric Schmitt, "Absence of Pity," *The Quill*, July/Aug. 1984, p.10.

3. Gene Goodwin, "The Ethics of Compassion," *The Quill*, Nov. 1983, p.39.

4. W.J. Cash, *The Mind of the South* (Knopf, New York, 1957), p.284.

5. Steve Neal, *Dark Horse*, (Doubleday, Garden City, N.Y., 1984), p.38.

6. Ellsworth Barnard, "The Private Life of a Public Figure," in *Wendell Willkie: Fighter for Freedom* (Northern Michigan University Press, Marquette, Mich., 1966), p.19.

7. Neal, *Dark Horse*, p.145.

8. Ralph Izard, "Judgment Issues Split Respondents," *1983 Journalism Ethics Report*, prepared by the National Ethics Committee, Society of Professional Journalists, Sigma Delta Chi, p.5.

9. Ibid., pp.5–6.

10. Rita Wolf, Tommy Thomason, and Paul LaRocque, "The Right to Know vs. the Right of Privacy: Newspaper Identification of Crime Victims," *Journalism Quarterly*, vol. 64, nos.2 and 3, Summer/Autumn 1987, pp.503–7.

11. Norbert Wiener, *The Human Use of Human Beings* (Doubleday, Garden City, N.Y., 1954), p.127.

12. David A. Anderson, "Crime Victims: Do They Have Privacy Rights?" in *Crime Victims and The News Media*, a report of a symposium Nov. 18, 1986, published by the *Fort Worth Star-Telegram* and Capital Cities/ABC Inc. Foundation.

13. Suggested by Marlene Young, executive director of the National Organization for Victim Assistance, and published in *News Media and Victims of Crime*, proceedings of a conference at New York University, Nov. 13, 1985.

14. William L. Rush and The League of Human Dignity, *Write with Dignity:*

Reporting on People with Disabilities, a Gilbert M. and Martha H. Hitchcock Center publication, School of Journalism, 206 Avery Hall, University of Nebraska, Lincoln, Neb., 68588–0127, pp.4–5.

15. Arthur L. Caplan, "Doctor's Duty Is to Protect Privacy of AIDS Victims," *Minneapolis Star and Tribune*, Aug. 9, 1987, p.21A. The apparent slowness with which society responded to AIDS is the theme of *And the Band Played On: Politics, People and the AIDS Epidemic* by Randy Shilts (St. Martin's Press, New York, 1987).

16. Mike Pride, "A Grieving Concord Repelled by Media Misbehavior," *presstime*, Mar. 1986, pp.12–13.

17. Roy Peter Clark, "Covering Crime: Journalists Face Difficult Choices," in *Crime Victims and the News Media*, p.5.

18. Ibid.

19. Jeff Greenfield, *An Abusive Press*, published by the Gannett Center for Media Studies, Columbia University, from remarks to the Colorado Press Association, Feb. 20, 1987.

Index